WAGNER'S
RING:

M. OWEN LEE

TURNING
THE SKY
ROUND

SUMMIT BOOKS

NEW YORK · LONDON · TORONTO · SYDNEY · TOKYO · SINGAPORE

SUMMIT BOOKS
Simon & Schuster Building
Rockefeller Center
1230 Avenue of the Americas
New York, New York 10020

Copyright © 1990 by M. Owen Lee
All rights reserved
including the right of reproduction
in whole or in part in any form.
SUMMIT BOOKS and colophon are
trademarks of Simon & Schuster Inc.
Designed by Edith Fowler
Manufactured in the United States of America

10 9 8 7 6 5 4 3 2 1

Library of Congress Cataloging in Publication Data

Lee, M. Owen
    Wagner's Ring : turning the sky round /
    M. Owen Lee.
        p.   cm.
    Based on the author's Metropolitan Opera
    intermission radio talks.
    Includes bibliographical references (p.
    Discography: p.
    I. Wagner, Richard, 1813–1883. Ring des Nibelungen.
    II. Title.
ML410.W15L3   1990
782.1—dc20   90–9489
ISBN 0–671–70773–6   CIP
                                                    MN

FOR
EDWARD DOWNES

Contents

Preface

"THE BASIS of this book is a series of radio intermission talks given in the United States of America during the broadcasts, sponsored by Texaco, of Wagner's *Ring* cycle from the Metropolitan Opera, New York."

Those words, the opening sentence of a book published almost fifteen years ago by the late John Culshaw, can also serve to introduce the volume you have in your hand. For this book began, as did his eloquent *Reflections on Wagner's Ring*, as four intermission commentaries broadcast live from the Met.

Audience response to those commentaries was remarkable. Hundreds of requests for copies came to me, from almost every one of the United States, from most of the provinces of Canada, even from Europe. They came from professional musicians and professors of music, from academics in university departments of art, literature, psychology, and science, from the various professions as well as from the general public. (I hasten to add that Mr. Culshaw received at least as great a response to *his* talks, and that the inimitable Boris Goldovsky, through his close to fifty years on the intermissions, may well have drawn the largest response of all. The Metropolitan broadcasts can reach a radio audience of some eight million people, and most of those listeners are eager to learn and uncommonly responsive.)

The four intermission features of April 1, 8, 15, and 22, 1989, form the Introduction and chapters two, three, and four of this book. Chapter one is based on another intermission talk I gave, on *Das Rheingold*, from the Met during the previous season, on January 16, 1988. All five appear here in much the same form as on the broadcasts. There has been some rewriting to render them suitable for a reading, rather than a listening, public. There has been some simplification in the matter of musical examples, which are keyed in the text to an index at the back of the book. And the talks themselves are somewhat longer than they were on the air, as all five were trimmed to the second— sometimes hastily at the last second—to make them fit into the time available at intermission.

The tailoring was done at the sensible insistence of Mr. Richard Mohr, the producer of the broadcast intermissions. I should like to thank him here for making helpful suggestions before and for sitting at my elbow during those tense on-the-air moments in List Hall. And of course I must extend my thanks to Texaco as well. In that I am joined by millions of people who, across some fifty years, have had their lives enriched on Saturday afternoons when, as Milton Cross used to say, "Texaco presents the Metropolitan Opera."

On the broadcasts, Mr. Cross and, in recent years, Peter Allen have filled the listening audience in on the plots of the afternoon operas. That has left intermission commentators like me free to speak about subplots and subtexts. For the purposes of this volume, however, I have been encouraged to include plot summaries of the four parts of the *Ring*. They are my own, and I hope that readers will not find them too idiosyncratic. I thought that, if summaries were needed, they ought to be different from those to be had in a hundred other books. Certainly I thought it more important to say that Siegfried and Brünnhilde end their love duet laughing at the impending destruction of the world (a significant detail that I've never seen in a plot synopsis) than to say that Sieglinde gives Hunding a sleeping potion (a less-than-significant plot device that seems to appear in every synopsis but mine).

I have added as well what I hope will be a helpful guide to further reading on Wagner, and a few suggestions for home listening to (and, in this age of videocassettes and laser discs, home viewing of) Wagner's inexhaustible myth in music. For what is true in the pages I have written I am greatly indebted to both the books and the records I have cited.

Some of what I said on the air appeared earlier, in different form, in two articles—"Wagner's *Ring*: Turning the Sky Round," in *The Opera Quarterly* for Summer 1983, and "Out of the Woods" (not, I must say, a title I suggested) in *Opera News* for February 27, 1988. I am grateful to both publications for allowing me to reprint the material here. I should also like to thank, for their help in getting this book into print, Margaret Carson, Ileene Smith, and Alan Williams and, for their encouragement over the years, Frank Merkling,

Dorothy Graziani, William Lonsdale, Irene Sloan, Vinnie Volpe, Michael Keenan, and perhaps most of all the hundreds who wrote from the radio audience.

Many of those who wrote had reasons not to like Wagner, or rather not to like what Wagner has often come to mean. Some of them had fled from the horrors of Nazi Germany. Some had lost loved ones there. One had even survived the terrible bombing of Dresden. And yet they remembered Wagner as much more than the monster he has been thought to be and in his private life, to some extent, was. They realized that our greatest artists are profoundly ambivalent men and women, and can be read in diverse and even opposed ways. They felt, and often said eloquently in their letters, that there was something in Wagner that they found nowhere else, something that touched them deeply and consoled them for their hurt and loss. Hearing Wagner on the air in America took those who had fled from Europe back, wondering, to painful memories of the past but also, wondering still more, to happy memories of family music rooms and afternoons in opera parterres and galleries. I was moved by those letters and, though I answered them as well as I could as they reached me, I want to take this occasion to thank the many people who have thanked me.

In this last decade of our century we are coming to see Wagner as a man who has influenced profoundly many aspects of contemporary thought and feeling. For a hundred years he has cast a spell on post-Romantic and twelve-tone composers, stream-of-consciousness novelists, impressionist painters, and imagist poets. The staging of his works has

continued to affect modern theater. He laid the
groundwork for the structural analysis of myth. More
than that, he anticipated the findings of this century's
new science, psychiatry. He was the forerunner of
those who have, as he predicted they would, "made
the unconscious conscious." He was one of the first to
see the psyche's potential for creation and destruction, and in his mature music dramas he called for the
healing of its warring contents. He was, perhaps like
all artists in proportion to their greatness, prophetic.
In the *Ring* and *Die Meistersinger* and *Parsifal* he told
us that we are headed for world destruction if we
cannot evolve a political system that does not use
money for power, if we cannot develop an ethical
system that recognizes and contravenes our self-
destructive urges, if we cannot learn to love.

The unconvinced (and I must be honest and
admit that I have heard from one or two of them, too)
continue to point out that the very solutions Wagner
called for in humankind at large he was unable to find
in himself. But that, as Hans Sachs sings so memora-
bly in *Die Meistersinger*, is why the artist creates—out
of the abundance of his own need. Like his Wotan and
his Sachs and his Amfortas, Wagner needed healing.
It is not too much to say that what he couldn't achieve
in his life he did achieve in his art, which is a celebration of the completeness we all hope to find in the lives
given us to lead. Ultimately the self-absorbed Wagner
wrote for all of us.

These are ideas I have thought through with the
man to whom this book is gratefully dedicated—a
musician who loves and understands Wagner as few
of us can hope to do, and a friend who often takes me

home after a Met broadcast to a glass of port, a steaming hot stew, and an evening of civilized conversation. To him I say, as the grateful Pogner said to the man who helped him understand what he loved, "O Sachs, mein Freund! Wie dankenswert!"

Introduction

CAN YOU REMEMBER when you first felt the power of music? The scholar C. S. Lewis, who sometimes wrote stories for children, once looked back on his own childhood, in a book he called *Surprised by Joy*, and he told there how he first awakened to Wagner. It was intuitive and instantaneous. "I can lay my hand on the very moment," he said. "There is hardly any fact I know so well."

Lewis was a boy in an English schoolroom when he first saw Arthur Rackham's illustrations for Wagner's *Ring*. "'The sky had turned round,'" he remembered. "Pure 'Northernness' engulfed me: a vision of huge, clear spaces hanging above the Atlantic in the endless twilight . . . and almost at the same moment I knew that I had met this before, long, long ago . . . There arose at once, almost like heartbreak, the memory of Joy itself, the knowledge that I had once had what I had now lacked for years, that I was returning at last from exile and desert lands to my own country . . . I stared round that dusty schoolroom like a man recovering from unconsciousness . . . and at once I knew (with fatal knowledge) that to have [that sense] again was the supreme and only important object of desire."

To recapture that sense, young Lewis found and read "in rapture" a synopsis of the *Ring*, and then he wrote a long schoolboy's poem on it, and finally he heard, in a crowded gramophone shop, his first excerpt from Wagner's *Ring*—the Ride of the Valkyries. "From that moment," he says, "Wagnerian records became the chief drain on my pocket money and the presents I invariably asked for. 'Music' was one thing, 'Wagnerian music' quite another, and there was no common measure between them. It was . . . a new kind of pleasure, if indeed 'pleasure' is the right word, rather than trouble, ecstasy, astonishment, 'a conflict of sensations without name.'"

I quote from C. S. Lewis, and at some length, because he describes an experience, an awakening, most of us who love Wagner have felt, and may have felt earlier than our teens: a sense that in discovering Wagner we have discovered something no other music has, something in ourselves we knew long before but had forgotten. I also cite Lewis because he came to Wagner, first through an intuitive idea associated with land- and sky- and seascape, then through graphic illustrations, then through the story of the *Ring*, and finally and most overwhelmingly through the music itself. He calls it all "a conflict of sensations without name," but Wagner, who had a name for it— *Gesamtkunstwerk*, the work of art that affects us at some deep personal level through a conflux of idea, the plastic arts, poetry, and music—Wagner would say, "Yes, that is very much as I intended."

And Wagner, who is said sometimes to turn us

unhealthily inward, opened young Lewis outward to the world: "I was always involuntarily looking," he says, "for scenes that might belong to the Wagnerian world, here a steep hillside covered with firs where Mime might meet Sieglinde, there a sunny glade where Siegfried might listen to the bird, or presently a dry valley of rocks where the lithe scaly body of Fafner might emerge from its cave." Years later he recalled, "It seemed to me that I had tasted heaven then"—a final reason for citing Lewis: for him Wagner was not limiting but liberating. Wagner provided the young scholar with the insight—the memory, the visionary gleam of joy—that eventually took him through the Great War, and reading "Greats" and teaching philosophy at Oxford, to the sense of God that irradiates all his work.

Is there anything, in all the realm of art, to set beside _Der Ring des Nibelungen_? This cycle of four immense music dramas, the vastest piece of music ever conceived by the mind of man—what an experience it is first to discover, and then to spend a lifetime exploring, those four parts, tracing their connective links, puzzling out their meanings, and listening through in wonder and awe to their shattering conclusion!

At the start, the _Ring_ may seem like some kind of children's story, a fanciful tale set in a land of long ago. It is easy, too, to see it as a myth about nature—a very contemporary statement about man's greedy, insane exploitation of nature, and about the impending threat of the world's annihilation. Then, after a few hearings, it comes to seem mythic in the deepest sense: it uses external nature to tell us about our inner selves. But Wagner, when he began it, seems to have intended the *Ring* as a political allegory for his own century. And that is the way we will consider it first.

Some ten years before a note of the *Ring* was penned, while the German states were struggling to make of themselves a kind of united states, several prominent men of letters, among them Franz Brendel and Friedrich Theodor Vischer, saw the need for a national opera based on one of Germany's ancestral myths. They suggested as the ideal subject the twelfth-century *Nibelungenlied*.

Many people who know Wagner well have, I find, an incorrect view of the *Nibelungenlied*. It is a far cry from the *Ring*. It is a twelfth-century Middle High German epic set up and down the Rhine and the Danube in the Christian Middle Ages, climaxing in the cathedral city of Worms. It contains no gold stolen from water nymphs, no scenes in Valhalla, no earth-flooding, heaven-firing catastrophe, and no redemption of the world by love. Its Siegfried is not a hero of divine descent by way of an incestuous marriage, but only a well-bred young Rhinelander with magic cloak and treasure hoard, a guileless warrior who marries into Burgundian royalty and is stabbed in the back. The Brünnhilde of the *Nibelungenlied* is not a Valkyrie sent to summon heroes from the battlefield, but only an Icelandic virago forced to marry into the same dastardly Burgundian family. The destruction at the end is sent not by cosmic forces but by the wrathful Kriemhild, the character Wagner calls Gutrune, at the eastern palace of Attila the Hun.

The *Nibelungenlied* is a medieval Christian version of what had once been an old pagan cycle of myths. Though it is one of the best of all medieval sagas, a long and flavorsome poem crowded with incident, it appears only to half-understand the old myths it has adapted, and it fits those myths into a sometimes alien twelfth-century context. All the same, it was the *Nibelungenlied* that nineteenth-century intellectuals thought would serve as the basis for a new kind of opera.

The *Nibelungenlied* was translated into modern German for the first time when Wagner was a boy, and in new translations it suddenly found interested readers all over Europe. The Englishman Thomas Carlyle called it "our northern *Iliad*," and urged all northern Europeans to see in its heroic opposition to materialism a vision that might save industrialized Europe from the power-mad, wealth-seeking course on which it was bent. Carlyle saw "the curse of gold" as the central theme of the old poem, and he saw his Europe as laboring under that same curse.

At least two other composers of note— Schumann and Mendelssohn—thought about turning the *Nibelungenlied* into an opera, and Wagner's rival Heinrich Dorn actually produced a *Die Nibelungen* in 1854. The idea for the *Ring*, then, did not spring full-grown and armed, like Athene from the brain of Zeus, from Wagner's endlessly seething, outsized head. Nor was the *Nibelungenlied* going to be enough for him. He had already dramatized medieval German legends in *Tannhäuser* and *Lohengrin*, and wanted to get back to the *pre*-medieval pagan sources of *these* legends.

So he went past the *Nibelungenlied* to the earlier prose and verse Eddas, to the Thidriks Saga and the Völsunga Saga—more Norse than German, but reaching back to a pagan pan-Germanic source. In all of these, Wagner isolated those parts that seemed to him of most significance, re-arranged them for maximum impact, and added details not in the sources. Only in Wagner, for example, does the dwarf Alberich steal the gold guarded at the bottom of the Rhine by three water spirits; only in Wagner does the omniscient earth mother Erda appear; only in Wagner does the sky god's daughter Brünnhilde come to the hero Siegmund to announce his death. In fact, the more one rummages about in the sources, the more one comes to see that the best mythic ideas in the *Ring* emerged from Wagner's own imagination—one of the greatest testaments to his genius.

Now if the medieval *Nibelungenlied* was a mine of mythic symbolism for northern Europeans seeking their roots, even more were those older pagan sagas, with their mist-wrapped northern gods. In Wagner's *Lohengrin*, pagan Ortrud stands before a Christian cathedral and calls for the return of those gods. And in Wagner's day they did return. They started replacing Greek Zeus and Roman Jupiter in schoolchildren's books in German- and English-speaking lands. Even Bible stories were being crowded out by tales of Odin and Thor and Sigurd.

The rising of new myths, or the re-appearance of old ones, even in children's books, reflects important changes in society. And indeed Europe *was* changing. The Latin countries began to view the developments east of the Rhine and north of the Alps with some alarm. One famous German left the town where my grandfather was born, crossed the Rhine, and went into self-imposed exile in France, the better to contemplate what was happening in his own country. In 1834, as L. J. Rather records for us, that prophetic

German issued a warning. France might think that its German neighbors were a stolid, orderly, peaceful lot, only a little dreamy perhaps. Actually, a spiritual earthquake of extraordinary magnitude was, he said, slowly building up in German lands. A catastrophe would come in comparison with which the French Revolution would seem like a harmless idyll. The old gods would arise and rub the dust of a thousand years from their eyes. Thor would spring up with his giant hammer and smash the Gothic cathedrals. The *furor Teutonicus*, the berserk madness of the ancient Northmen, would stalk across Europe and the world.

Heinrich Heine, famous for his imaginative powers as well as for his ironic gifts, was saying in startling and picturesque terms from Latin Europe what Carlyle was saying more matter-of-factly from Anglo-Saxon Europe: the old Europe was finished; the established interests of the past—blood, title, property, religion, all now bent to shore up a corrupt industrialist-capitalist society—would be replaced by something closer to nature. Heine was, however, more concerned than Carlyle about the new forces getting out of control. And of course, they did.

During the Franco-Prussian War, Heine's Thor was Bismarck. During World War I, he was Kaiser Wilhelm perhaps, and during World War II, Hitler surely. But the prophecy could as easily apply to more than military conquest. It could apply to Karl Marx, whose revolutionary thought has since claimed a third of the world's population. Such was the power of the re-emergence of the old Germanic myths.

Wagner was one of the first to sense the wider implications of the myths. And he was increasingly convinced that it was the theater's purpose to dramatize for a people its mythic heritage, and thereby show them themselves. He spent a lot of time reading, and reading about, the dramatists of ancient Greece, whose purpose it was to represent to their people the great ancestral myths. Some of what I have called Wagner's own contributions to the Nibelung stories may actually have come out of his reading of the Greeks. Aeschylus had dramatized the primeval theft of an elemental power, fire, in his Prometheus cycle. Greek myths had spoken of an earth mother, Gaea, as the oldest of nature's divinities, and of a warrior goddess, Athene, as the embodiment of the father god's wisdom. These mythic notions are only slightly changed in Wagner's *Ring*. Certainly it became Wagner's burning desire to dramatize for his Germany, as Aeschylus had for his Greece, the myths that were primitive man's first ways of understanding himself.

As the Nibelung subject began to shape itself in Wagner's mind, Siegfried seemed to be the figure most useful for his purposes. Siegfried could be made into a hero whose tragic death would serve as a redemptive act through which the whole world is cleansed from the curse of wealth and power. At first, Wagner concentrated all the Nibelung myths into one single drama called "Siegfried's Death."

The year he started all of this, 1848, was a year of political uprisings in Paris, Vienna, and Berlin. The thirty-four-year-old Wagner was actually sketching a quite different opera that year, on Frederick Barbarossa. He also thought, that year, about adapting the myth of Achilles. Then he turned to the German version of the myth of the artist Daedalus. Finally he produced a fifty-two-page outline for a drama called—

"Jesus of Nazareth." All of this along with the Siegfried project!

I think he had picked up an idea advanced most notably at the time by Hegel. In his *History of Philosophy* (published posthumously in 1834) Hegel had said, "This is the role of heroes in the history of mankind: it is through them that a new world comes into being." With heroes like Achilles and Siegfried and Jesus, whole peoples move into new areas of awareness. For Hegel, a hero is a mythic figurehead, a symbol of the aspiration of the race as it evolves. This is very much what Wagner wanted to dramatize, and, for a while, each successive hero seemed best for his purposes. He finally opted for Siegfried as his evolutionary force.

Wagner thought he saw something of Siegfried in a non-German, Mikhail Bakunin, a burly and extroverted Russian anarchist who had known Marx and Engels. One night in Dresden, after Wagner had conducted Beethoven's Ninth, Bakunin came up to him and said, in a low roar, that if all the other music ever written were destroyed in the fire that would soon consume the world, Beethoven's Ninth ought to be saved, even if they had to die for it. Bakunin's prediction of the coming revolution in Russia sounded like a Götterdämmerung indeed: the peasant class, naturally good, would set fire to the palaces of its imperial oppressors, and all of civilization would, if it came to that, go under. Authorities in Dresden began to look on Wagner, state employee though he was, with alarm—so often was he seen with Bakunin and with another revolutionary, the young conductor August Röckel.

Bakunin thought Wagner's quieter views on what was going to happen in Europe hopelessly naive. In the first draft of "Siegfried's Death," Wagner ends with the sky god Wotan (that is to say, the Saxon king) receiving Siegfried into that Germanic heaven, Valhalla, while the world below is made a kind of classless republic. (Wagner's final version, of course, was not to be that simple.)

In May of the next year, the revolutionary uprisings spread to Dresden. Wagner was in the thick of them—providing places for secret meetings, assuming publication of a banned political journal, supplying grenades, haranguing the insurgents at the barricades, reporting on troop movements from the steeple of the Kreuzkirche, and watching the opera house where he was employed go up in smoke. At last it was as if his hopes were being fulfilled: now revolution would sweep the masses into power, and a new culture would spread across Europe, nourished by that other plan that buzzed, alongside political revolution, in his head—a new German national theater. (No marks for guessing who would be the dramatist.)

But Prussian troops poured into Dresden to quell the revolution, and Wagner fled to Franz Liszt, in Weimar. It was as well he got out of Saxony. His friends Bakunin and Röckel were arrested and sentenced to death—though the sentences were later commuted to long prison terms. Liszt calmed Wagner down sufficiently to get him started on the music for "Siegfried's Death," and the disillusioned revolutionary tampered with the ending of his text, indicating that the god Wotan (that is to say, the Saxon king) was responsible for the injustices in the world.

Then, under Saxon edict, Wagner found that he

had to flee Germany entirely. With a price on his head, and letters back to his distraught wife, Minna, and a symbolic stop at the Wartburg (where earlier German rebels like Tannhäuser and Luther had found sanctuary) he got to Zurich (where later exiles like Lenin were to find sanctuary). And the ending to his "Siegfried's Death" changed again. In the new, third ending, the guilty Wotan will no longer rule the world. He is told to "depart forever," to "fade away."

But that was never set to music. In fact, Wagner now wrote no music for close to six years. Instead, he put down on paper the hundreds of ideas fermenting in him, in that notorious stream of books, articles, and pamphlets that included *Art and Revolution*, "Man and Existing Society," *The Art of the Future*, and *Opera and Drama*.

When his interest in the Siegfried project picked up again, Wagner saw that he had to preface his "Siegfried's Death" with a preliminary drama, "Young Siegfried." The text for that came quickly, in a matter of weeks. Then that, too, needed a preface. With growing excitement, and frequent excursions into Switzerland's awesome mountain regions, Wagner sketched "Siegmund and Sieglinde," about Siegfried's parents. And then he drafted yet another drama, "The Theft of the Rhine Gold," to set before that. So he wrote his four texts in reverse order. The *Ring* became a tetralogy, though for years Wagner spoke of it as a trilogy—three operas with a prologue. (He was still claiming the mantle of Aeschylus, who had shaped the massive myths of Greece into trilogies.)

Wagner also began to realize that his Siegfried

project was now so vast it could only be performed over several days, at some sort of festival. (That notion too was Greek.)

And when he saw his four parts as a whole, Wagner changed the ending again—and made a really remarkable change. He decided to introduce into his drama something that had never been part of the Siegfried myths before—the old Norse Ragnarök, the myth of the twilight of the gods. This was a doomsday myth in which gods and heroes battle with the powers of evil, and all the combatants on both sides are destroyed, along with mankind, in a stupendous apocalyptic fire and flood. Wagner used as much of this as he could, saving most of the description for the music yet to come.

Clearly his *Ring* was becoming more than a socialist's political allegory. Wagner's intuition had led him to introduce the world-destruction myth, and he himself was not sure why. Like those novelists who tell us that their characters "take over" the writing and determine their own fates, Wagner acknowledged that his *Ring* was shaping itself from some source beyond his conscious control. Something was stirring in him that had to be said, no matter how. He didn't understand it. All he knew was that he had to complete it and, if need be, build a theater to present it. And it was to be something the like of which had not been seen on any stage since classic Greece and perhaps not even then: the problems of his Germany and his Europe and his century were to be objectified in, projected into a mythic, elemental world. To encompass this, Wagner felt intuitively that his hero-myth was not enough. Hegel had said that a hero's mission was to bring a new world into existence. Wagner *had* to introduce the whole world, and transform it.

In 1853, after five years of writing only words, and not a note of music, Wagner published the text. It was now called *Der Ring des Nibelungen*, and all four dramas were re-titled as we now know them, placed in their familiar order—*Das Rheingold*, *Die Walküre*, *Siegfried*, and *Götterdämmerung*. And that same eventful year, 1853, when Verdi produced *Il Trovatore* and *La Traviata*, Wagner began setting his *Ring* to music. He started now with the last text written but the first in the sequence, *Das Rheingold*, and proceeded forward. The music of the prelude to *Rheingold*, which sounds like the world evolving from primordial matter in the river's depth, came to him with overwhelming force. After a silence of almost six years, he was composing again, and as if at the sources of inspiration. The music flooded in on him.

So the cycle that ends with the world ending begins with the world beginning.

The *Ring* contains some fifteen hours of virtually continuous music. But it is bigger in every way than the mere number of hours and days it lasts. And it repays every effort to understand it. Most listeners respond first to its visions of river, mountains, storms, and rainbows, as young C. S. Lewis did. Perhaps they are "surprised by joy" and a hundred other feelings—and may even recall that somewhere, long, long ago, they heard all this before, and feel that in hearing it again they are somehow re-discovering themselves. For eventually we who listen to the *Ring* come to see that it is not, on its deepest levels, about the nine-

teenth or the twentieth or any one century. It took a
while even for Wagner to see that it takes place
outside of time, in the human imagination and the
memory.

In your imagination and memory. On the landscape of your soul, as you listen.

WAGNER'S RING

1
Das Rheingold

SCENE 1: *In the depths of the Rhine, three alluring water nymphs guard a golden treasure. The dwarf Alberich, one of the Nibelungs from the depths of the earth, pursues these Rhine maidens with amorous intent but without success. They tease and taunt him, and unwisely tell him that anyone who renounces love and fashions a ring from their gold will have power over the world. The dwarf promptly renounces love and steals the gold.*

SCENE 2: *On a mountain peak above the Rhine, the giants Fasolt and Fafner have built a castle, Valhalla, for the one-eyed father god Wotan, his wife Fricka, and their dynasty of sky gods. The giants expect as payment for their efforts one of the dynasty, the love goddess Freia. But Wotan, wielding a great ashen spear that bears inscribed the treaties that give him his power, is loath to give up Freia, for her golden apples keep the gods eternally youthful. Prompted by the fire god Loge, he offers as an alternative payment the gold that Alberich has stolen from the Rhine. The giants take Freia hostage till Wotan can secure the gold for them. The sky gods feel their youth and strength fading away with the loss of Freia.*

SCENE 3: *Wotan and Loge descend to the subterraneous caverns where Alberich, empowered by the Ring he has fashioned from the gold, keeps his fellow Nibelungs enslaved,*

*making additional wonders from the treasure. One of these
wonders is the Tarnhelm, a helmet that can grant its wearer
invisibility, instant transportability, and the power of meta-
morphosis. Wotan and Loge learn of this marvel from
Alberich's enslaved brother Mime. The two gods humor
Alberich into staging a transformation or two and, when he
assumes the form of a toad, take him captive easily, and
ascend with him to the upper world.*

SCENE 4: *Alberich is forced to summon his minions to haul
the whole of his golden treasure before the sky gods. Wotan
wrests the Ring from the dwarf's finger, puts it on his own,
and tells Loge to let the captive dwarf go. Alberich, before he
departs, puts a mighty curse on the Ring: death to all who
wear it, envy to those who do not.*

*The giants return with Freia and accept the gold as
alternative payment. They also claim the Tarnhelm and—
when the wise earth goddess Erda appears to persuade Wotan
to relinquish it—the Ring itself. The curse on the Ring
begins to work immediately, as the giants quarrel over it.
Fafner kills Fasolt and packs off with the golden hoard.
Wotan is shaken by Erda's stern prediction that the world he
rules will soon end, but contents himself for the moment with
his new sky castle. The thunder god Donner summons a
storm, and his brother Froh creates a rainbow bridge whereby
they, Freia, Fricka, and Wotan can cross the Rhine and enter
Valhalla. Loge, as fire god not part of Wotan's airy family,
predicts that the Valhallans are walking to their doom. In the
Rhine below, the nymphs lament the loss of their gold. The
four elements of earth, air, fire, and water are thus at
variance. A theme in the orchestra tells us Wotan has
conceived a plan to save the future—a sword.*

THE SUBJECT of Wagner's *Ring* is not much less than the world itself, the world projected in myth and music. All of external nature is in the cycle—pure, timeless nature and nature clouded and confounded. And our human nature is there too—all the storms and calms that we know within us, in our conscious and unconscious selves. I know of no other opera, or set of operas, perhaps even no other work of art, that looks outward and inward so astonishingly. The *Ring* gives us a special insight into the world and ourselves, and I would like now to try to define it.

One of the great questions that concerned the first philosophers, on their Greek islands, was the problem of the one and the many. As they thought their way past myth and into science, the pre-Socratics developed the idea that there was one unifying substance underlying all the multiple appearances in the world.

Wagner's *Ring* begins with a single E flat deep in the orchestra, hardly audible at first. Then a B flat hovers over it for several bars. And eventually the sound evolves into an arpeggioed E-flat major chord [example 1].*

Wagner told Franz Liszt that that opening music represented "the beginning of the world." Commentators have called it the *Motiv des Urelementes*, the motif of the primal element—of nature not yet separated into the elements of earth, air, fire, and water. But soon the theme is quickened by orchestral undulations. The unidentifiable substance evolves into water, the element that the first of the philosophers, Thales, said was the source of all things [example 2]. Then the theme picks up speed and color and feeling. We are in specific waters—the depths of the Rhine.

*Examples are keyed to the index of musical terms beginning on p. 113.

On one level, Wagner's *Ring* is about nature—about the cosmic struggles of its four elements, represented by gods, and the myriad moods of its changes, about its storms and calms, its primeval majesties, and above all its processes of evolution, its transformation of itself into all things and eventual resolution of all things back into itself.

There is evolution in the music even more than in the text. There are some two hundred musical themes, Leitmotifs, in the *Ring*, but—as Wagner quietly remarked, and as the English musicologist Deryck Cooke has since taught us to see—they all derive from a few basic motifs: those connected with unconscious nature and those connected with conscious man, the only one of nature's creatures to separate himself from her stream of unconsciousness.

The clearest example of this is the theme of the primal element itself. It is the source not only of the *Ring*'s water motifs, but also of the themes associated with earth. The motif that, in *Das Rheingold*, accompanies the appearance, out of the earth, of the primeval goddess Erda [example 3] is a minor variant of example 1. So too is the motif that, later in the *Ring*, describes earth's age-old ash tree. Musically, the primal element brings forth both water and earth, and from them, all things.

More than that, when the earth goddess Erda appears, she brings the implacable message that all things will eventually come to an end. Even the elemental gods will someday fade away in a Götterdämmerung, and die. The theme associated with that prophecy is, simply but powerfully, the primal nature theme inverted, nature calling back her own [example 4].

If water and earth are both manifestations of one underlying, undifferentiated substance, then we ought not to be surprised if, in the sparkling, pristine world Wagner conjures up, there are musical correspondences between water and earth, river and forest. There are in fact some astonishing correspondences between the music of the scene at the bottom of the Rhine that begins the *Ring* and that of the Forest Murmurs scene about halfway through the cycle, in Act II of *Siegfried*. The music that, in *Rheingold*, suggests the radiance of the waters [example 5] is all but echoed in the sound that depicts, in *Siegfried*, the murmurings in the forest [example 6]. The exultant cry of the creatures in the *Rheingold* waters [example 7] is very like the sighing of the *Siegfried* trees [example 8].

The most remarkable of these correspondences comes with the song of the water nymphs at the beginning of *Rheingold* [example 9]. The words they sing, those first words of the *Ring*—"Weia, Waga! Woge du Welle, walle zur Wiege!"—are not, as is sometimes said, nonsense words. But they are a kind of baby-talk: "Wonder-waters! Wander, you wave, waft to the cradle!" Just as the music evolves out of its E-flat fundament, so the words gradually shape themselves out of alliterative patterns—the syllabic beginnings of the words "wonder," "wander," and "water." And this happens in Wagner's music and text while before our eyes the world of nature evolves from the cradle of the waves. The song of the Rhine maidens at the start of the *Ring* is a lullaby to the newborn world.

Astonishingly, in the parallel Forest Murmurs scene in *Siegfried*, where the boy hero is wondering about the mother he has never seen, there, note for note with the song of nature in the waters, changed only to fit the bright new context, is the song of nature in the trees, the melody sung by the woodbird [example 10]. The Forest Murmurs scene in *Siegfried* is a return, in innocence and sweetness, to the preternatural wonder of the River Waters scene at the opening of *Rheingold*. And as the music of the two scenes corresponds, so do the psychological undercurrents: in both scenes, the response to nature is associated with mother-longings. This may not register too strongly on us in *Das Rheingold*, but by the Forest Murmurs scene in *Siegfried* we have come to suspect that the whole cycle may be thought to take place, not just in the world without, but in the world within—in the psyche of the one who listens.

The music of the two scenes awakens something of ourselves within us, not just because it is beautifully composed, but because it is intuitively right. It intimates that man, in the beginning, was one with nature—with a maternal nature not yet corrupted, harmoniously and perfectly at one, even to the elemental fusion of water and earth.

In poetry the association of water and earth images, of the liquid and the vegetative, has always had this deeply emotive force. In the *Iliad*, Andromache, knowing that her Hector will be killed, weeps "blossoming tears." In the *Odyssey* Homer's great sea is, like a field, "unharvested." Horace's *Odes*, as I have pointed out to generations of students, are poems shot through with associated images of rivers and trees, wine and roses, springs and forests—all of them images of man's mortality. In the Psalms, the just man is a tree planted by running water, and the exiles hang up their harps on the aspens by the rivers of Babylon. In Wagner's *Tristan und Isolde*, she awaiting him hears the hunting horns, first as the rustling of the leaves, then as the splashing of the fountains, and he awaiting her imagines her coming across the sea, walking on waves of flowers. In *Die Meistersinger*, the hero, associated with Adam, adds verse on verse to his "Prize Song" as his beloved, whose name is Eve, appears to him under trees and beside a rippling stream.

We cannot but respond to these associations. There is something in us that still longs for lost innocence and union with nature. Northrop Frye, the dean of Canadian literary critics, sees this response of the imagination to a lost golden age as "the framework of all literature," and artists through the ages have used metaphor in an attempt to reclaim it. Our finest epic in English is called *Paradise Lost*.

So far in these considerations, we've spoken of external nature (or the inner psyche) as innocent and unaware of itself. But gleaming through the waters in the opening scene of *Rheingold* is a mysterious light, a kind of golden eye. Perhaps it is even the eye of father Rhine, for that is how his daughters, the Rhine maidens, describe it. It is the Rhine's gold, a wonderful symbol of the light of consciousness buried deep within unconscious waters [example 11]. At the end of *Das Rheingold* we hear another theme of conscious power latent within the unconscious. This is the theme of the sword that the father god, Wotan, will someday bestow on his chosen hero. It leaps through the rainbow music of the final scene, a shining idea just emerging from the unconscious of the father god. And as we expect, it is a variant of our other theme of

gold = consciousness

emerging light. Both motifs are formed from simple
major chords—the water father's gold [example 11]
and the sky father's sword [example 12].

This suggestion of consciousness buried deep
within what appears to be unconscious nature brings
us to a second great consideration of myth, religion,
and philosophy. At one stupendous evolutionary
moment in pre-history, one of nature's creatures separated himself from the unconscious flowing and
burgeoning of nature and became conscious of himself. Prometheus stole fire. Adam ate the apple. Man
sundered his bond with nature and set himself on a
course of conscious individuation. In his mythologies,
man has forever after felt guilt about that sundering.
For when he became conscious of himself, man was
able to choose between good and evil, and he realized
that he was flawed, striving for good but prone to evil.
He had taken a momentous step forward, but something in him, and in his myths, still longed for that
half-remembered union with unconscious nature,
that innocence lost long ago.

So it is that, very soon after Wagner's Rhine has
evolved before our wondering gaze, Alberich enters
to wrest consciousness from the waves. He steals
away the golden eye, and he uses it for evil. The Rhine
maidens' joyous cry [example 7] is made the theme of
the world's enslavement [example 13], which in sub-
sequent parts of the *Ring* becomes a terrifying musical
depiction of the effect of this original sin [example 14].
Only at the end of the *Ring*, in Brünnhilde's Immolation Scene, when all is righted at last, is that sin
absolved [example 15].

This theft from nature is nowhere to be found in
Wagner's sources—not in the *Nibelungenlied* or in the

prose and verse Eddas or in the Norse myth of world ending, the Ragnarök. In the *Ring* Wagner is reforging his German and Norse stories, aligning them with the creation and destruction and original-sin myths of world mythologies.

And he is feeling his way into new revelations. Why, if Alberich is evil, does a noble, unforgettable theme [example 16] sound when Alberich first hears that he must forswear human love in order to possess for himself the Rhine's gold? I think because the original sinners of myth are profoundly ambivalent figures. Their primal offenses bring evil into the world but have, ultimately, positive effects. Prometheus, stealing fire from heaven, helps mankind to know and to think, and learns through his suffering. Adam, eating from the tree of the knowledge of good and evil, commits a sin that the Church in her liturgy calls a *felix culpa*, a "happy fault," because it brought so wonderful a redeeming. The wresting of consciousness from nature is associated with guilt, but the step, the original sin, had to be taken if the human race was to break its bond with mothering nature, the bond that kept it unaware, unthinking, merely intuitive like the animals. The race thereafter could think, and know, and do good or evil. It was, for the first time, fully human. Hence the moving, mysterious quality of the theme Wagner gives his Alberich at his great moment of choice.

If, then, there is one fundamental insight that, intentionally or intuitively, underlies the *Ring*, it is that everything existent has evolved from one primal substance. And a second important idea is that man, to become man, had to separate himself from the rest of nature by evolving out of it into a conscious state of being—or, as the myths seem always to picture it, by wresting consciousness from nature.

So Wagner's *Ring* raises the great questions thinking man has asked—questions about a dimly remembered universal creation and a fearfully anticipated universal destruction, questions about the fallibility of human nature, and the breakthrough that occurred when, at some moment, man separated himself from nature and began his conscious life.

No one interpretation can adequately encompass a work so vast as the *Ring*, and there is something to be said for modern productions that set it, not amid pristine rivers and trees, but in the nineteenth century amid the industrial and other revolutions, or in some corrupt twentieth-century metropolis, or amid some future star wars. But these are all, in the end, limiting concepts. The best productions set the *Ring* in the timeless pre-history Wagner set it in. And if my remarks seem remote from most of the *Ring*s to be seen today from Salzburg to Seattle, perhaps we should let Wagner speak: "From the moment when man perceived the difference between himself and nature, and so began his own development as man by breaking loose from the unconsciousness of natural animal existence and passing over into conscious life—when he therefore set himself in opposition to nature and developed the faculty of thought—from that moment error began, as the first expression of consciousness. But error," Wagner continues, "is the father of knowledge." And he concludes, "This is the history of the human race, from the myths of earliest times down to the present day."

Wagner also said, and I as a commentator must

take this to heart, "To make my intention too obvious would get in the way of real understanding." He didn't want explanations. He preferred to use what he called "the suggestive value of myth's symbols" so as to arrive at "the deep truths concealed within them." In his mythic works he wanted "to bring the unconscious part of human nature into consciousness." He was sure that there, in the human unconscious partially revealed in myth, we could learn the real truth about ourselves. He anticipated by a half century some of the discoveries of depth psychology. The last words of *Das Rheingold,* sung by the Rhine maidens, are "Tenderness and truth lie only in the depths. Everything above is harsh and false."

Those same words Wagner quoted the night before he died when, awake in the darkened house in Venice, he went to the piano and played the lament of the water creatures, "Rheingold, Rheingold."

"I am kind to them," he said as he returned to his room, "those creatures of the waters."

The next day, an all-knowing nature took back to herself the composer who had shown us some of the secrets in her depths.

2
Die Walküre

Act I: *In a forest storm, Wotan's mortal son, Sieg-mund, finds shelter, not knowing that he has come to the house of the very enemy he has been fleeing from, Hunding. He is befriended by Hunding's wife, the gentle Sieglinde, but he keeps his name from her. Hunding, according to primitive rites of hospitality, will shelter the fugitive for the night, then fight him in the morning. Siegmund is weaponless, and calls on his father, whom he knew only as a mortal named Wälse, for the sword he once promised to send in an hour of need. While Hunding sleeps, Sieglinde comes to Siegmund and points out a sword that a mysterious stranger had once thrust into a great ash tree. As Siegmund and Sieglinde fall in love, they realize, from twinship of face and voice, and from common parenthood under Wälse, that they are long-lost brother and sister. Sieglinde confers on Siegmund his rightful name. He pulls the foredestined sword from the ash tree, names it Nothung (need), claims his sister as his bride, and escapes with her.*

Act II: *Wotan, who began his plan for the future by assuming human guise as Wälse and siring the mortal twins Siegmund and Sieglinde, has also sired in his own name nine immortal angel-warrioresses, the Valkyries. Their role is to defend heroes in battle, to greet them before their deaths, and to gather them after death from the battlefields and bear them through the air on horseback to Valhalla. There, in an afterlife, the heroes will defend the sky god from attack.*

In a mountain gorge, Wotan tells his favorite Valkyrie daughter, Brünnhilde, whose mother is the intuitive Erda, that she must defend Siegmund in the coming encounter with Hunding. Fricka storms in to remind Wotan that his power rests on the contracts he has made with nature: if he defies his own laws and defends an incestuous hero, he will lose everything.

Wotan, alone with Brünnhilde, explains to her that she must disregard his former command. She must now see to it that Siegmund, his own son, dies at the hands of Hunding. And, he confides, when his own son is gone, a son of Alberich, just sired, will take possession of the Ring and the world.

Brünnhilde grieves that her father's mortal son must die, but she nonetheless obeys his command, and appears in epiphany to Siegmund to announce his impending death. Then Siegmund's brave devotion to Sieglinde so touches her that she disobeys her father and attempts to defend Siegmund in the duel with Hunding. Wotan furiously intervenes with his spear, smashes the sword he had left for his son, allows Hunding to kill Siegmund, then fells Hunding himself with a single word. Brünnhilde meanwhile has gathered up the pieces of the sword and rescued Sieglinde, who is to have Siegmund's child.

Act III: The Valkyries, en route to Valhalla with the bodies of slain heroes, land their horses on a mountaintop. Brünnhilde comes last to land, bringing Sieglinde, who hastens safely into the forest with the fragments of Siegmund's sword. Wotan appears in thunder, dismisses the other eight Valkyries, and sentences Brünnhilde, for her disobedience, to be reduced to mortal state and take as husband the first man

who wakens her from sleep. She pleads that she has only done
what she knew he wanted inwardly. He is moved, for what
she says is true. He promises that her slumber will be
surrounded by flames, so that only a great hero will waken
her. They both know that that hero will be Siegmund's child.
With great tenderness the father god kisses his daughter to
sleep and summons Loge to encircle her with a wall of magic
fire.

LATE IN THE YEAR 1853, when he had finished what he
called "the great scene in the *Rheingold*," Wagner
wrote to Franz Liszt, "My friend! I am in a state of
wonderment! A new world stands revealed before
me . . . everything within me seethes and makes
music. Oh, I am in *love!*"

We hear something of that exaltation in Act I of
Die Walküre. It's clearly the music of a man who felt the
joy of creation as he wrote. Listening to it, you would
hardly suppose that it was music adhering strictly to
severe, solidly reasoned principles. But it is. No other
act in Wagner observes so closely the principles Wagner had laid down, in his book *Opera and Drama*, as
essential to true musical theater. There he ruled that
the words had to share equally with the music in
realizing the drama; that the words should sound in
alliterative clusters; that the vocal line should spring
directly out of the rise and fall of the words; that the
singers should never blend their voices but give the
impression, while singing, of heightened speech; that
what the sung words could not say the orchestra
should say—in those ever-recurring musical themes
Wagner called "motifs of memory."

None of that sounds too promising, certainly not

to an opera-lover nursed on an Italian tradition of arias
and duets. But how wonderfully it all works out in the
first act of *Die Walküre!* What impassioned music
springs out of the archaic-sounding words! How me-
lodious the vocal line becomes, and how suspenseful
the action! And all the while the vast orchestra is
commenting on what we see, using musical motifs to
tell us what the characters do not say—and sometimes
do not even know.

Some of the recurring musical themes in this
second opera we have not heard before—the tender
motifs associated with Siegmund and Sieglinde and
their common parentage, and the menacing theme of
Hunding. But it is the music we already know from
Rheingold that comments most tellingly on the action
here. At the very start, the *Rheingold* motif of Wotan's
spear [example 17] is figured in the cellos and double
basses during the storm, changed but still recogniz-
able. It now sounds like the precipitous flight of a man
through the forest. To that man in flight the storm is
only a storm. But we who have heard *Das Rheingold*
can hear, in the man's desperate footsteps, the fore-
destining spear of his father, Wotan. We know that
there is a power and a plan at work as Siegmund flees
through the wind and rain. Wotan is with him.

The *Rheingold* motif of Wotan's sky castle, Valhalla [example 18] returns in *Walküre* when Sieglinde
tells Siegmund how a mysterious stranger came to her
unhappy wedding celebration, and thrust a sword
into an old ash tree. No one knew then who the
unknown figure was. But we can hear the Valhalla
motif in the horns as Sieglinde sings, and we know,
though she does not, that that awesome apparition
was her father, Wotan, and that his presence at the

wedding was, like his sending Siegmund through the storm, another part of his providential plan.

And when in *Rheingold* Wotan first conceived that plan, the orchestra sounded a motif for which there was not yet an association or a meaning [example 12]. In *Walküre*, when Siegmund is called to play his part in Wotan's evolving plan, and Sieglinde directs his eyes to the ash tree, the meaning of that motif is revealed. It signifies the sword that Wotan planted there, for the future.

And when in *Rheingold* Alberich was told he had to renounce love in order to possess the gold and win power over the world, a solemn theme [example 16] sounded, for Alberich was about to determine momentously the future of the world. In *Walküre*, when Siegmund pulls the sword from the tree, he intones that same motif, for he too has reached the critical moment in his life: he is beginning the plan of Wotan that will eventually restore the gold to its natural state and transform the world. Siegmund knows nothing of this. But we do, from the motif that recurs at that moment.

Then, about a half hour into the second act of *Walküre*, there is a change in the *Ring* music. The various motifs continue unabated as a comment on the words, but Wotan's music becomes quite palpably more introspective and pessimistic. At one point it almost comes to a halt. That is when the father god, alone with yet another of his children, the Valkyrie daughter Brünnhilde, looks into himself and realizes, in a long but fast-moving, half-whispered monologue, that his plan to dominate the world is doomed to failure.

By the time Wagner came to set that passage to

music, his view of the world had changed, even as his idealistic hopes for a new Europe had changed. Never again was he to be the wide-eyed revolutionary he had been in Dresden. He now saw that not only Germany, from which he was exiled, and not only Europe, of which he despaired, but the world itself was laboring under a curse from which there was no release.

What had happened? Wagner had read, for the first time, that philosophical tome of Arthur Schopenhauer called *The World as Will and Representation*. In fact, he read it through four whole times the year he was working on Act II of *Die Walküre*, and he returned to it often for the rest of his life.

What he read in Schopenhauer was profoundly pessimistic: the world we see is not reality but only our representation of reality. The ultimately real is a force we cannot see. Schopenhauer called it "will," *Wille*. This inscrutable power works in the cosmos far beyond us and also in the soul deep within each of us. The world, and we who are in the world, are driven towards goals which, once achieved, prove to be illusory and meaningless. Schopenhauer urged his readers to look steadily at this force that is the cause of all our suffering, to see it for what it is, to withdraw from it, and renounce it.

Suddenly, as he wrote the music for Act II of *Die Walküre*, Wagner thought he saw what his *Ring* really meant. His Europe, symbolized in the drama by Wotan's world, will never find release from its struggles, for endless, meaningless struggling is inherent in the very nature of that world. Wagner wrote to Liszt, "I looked at my poem and saw to my astonishment that what convinced me in Schopenhauer was already there, in my poetic concept. Only then did I really understand my Wotan. I was deeply moved. For years after that, Schopenhauer's book was never far from me. Its ever-growing influence on me and my life was extraordinary and decisive."

Wagner explained this further to his fellow revolutionary Röckel, still languishing in a Saxon prison: "I started my poem with an optimistic view of the world . . . and I hardly noticed, when I was outlining it, that I was unconsciously following a quite different and much more profound intuition. I was seeing, not a single moment in the world's evolution, but the essence of the world, the world in all of its moments." That is to say, the *Ring* was coming to represent not one nineteenth-century moment— industrialized Europe on the brink of political revolution—but the whole history of the world, from beginning to end, a world spun on endlessly and meaninglessly. Wagner henceforth all but dismissed the political element in his *Ring* ("a single moment in the world's evolution") in favor of a metaphysical meaning ("the essence of the world in all of its moments"). "And," Wagner continued, "I saw that the world was *Nichtigkeit*"—nothingness. An illusion.

He made this even more emphatic when he wrote to Liszt, "The world is *evil*, fundamentally evil!"

To make his *Ring* an illustration of Schopenhauer, Wagner hardly had to change his text. His poem was already shot through with references to Wotan's lost eye, Wotan's imperfect view of the world, and especially to Wotan's *Wille*. Writing the text, Wagner had intuitively anticipated Schopenhauer just as, commentators today are saying, he intuited in advance the discoveries of Freud and Jung.

Let's try now to understand further the lonely god whom Wagner, after reading Schopenhauer, began himself to understand: Wotan, all-Father, war-Father, a god who wills the destruction of the world he has ordered according to his will.

THE *RING* BEGINS in the depths of the Rhine, with Alberich stealing the Rhine's gold. But that isn't the earliest of Wagner's *Ring* myths. Before Alberich committed his crime against nature, Wotan was acting in the world. Through most of the *Ring*, Alberich appears to be the original sinner, the first to have wrested consciousness from nature. But by the fourth opera, *Götterdämmerung*, we hear confirmed what we long before came to suspect—that another, greater figure, before Alberich, committed a similar act and is also, for all his attempts at justice, a source of evil in the world. This, of course, is Wotan himself.

The orchestra tells us that there is a connection between the power of Alberich and the power of Wotan as early as the first change of scene in the *Ring*. Alberich's Ring, that symbol of consciousness, is represented musically in a curiously ambivalent, rounding theme [example 19]. Then, as the scene changes from the river's depths to the sky's heights, the Ring motif transforms itself gradually until we hear and see Wotan's newly fashioned, impregnable mountain castle, Valhalla [example 18]. The music implies that Wotan as well as Alberich is shaping nature into power for world domination.

And Wotan's was the real original sin, the first ambivalent wresting of consciousness from nature. That historian of Romanticism, Morse Peckham, once suggested that Wagner should have written yet a fifth opera, all about Wotan, and placed it before *Das Rheingold*, and called it *Die Weltesche*, "The World Ash Tree."

Let's make an opera here—*Die Weltesche*—out of information from Act II of *Die Walküre* and from the many flashback speeches of the operas yet to come.

Let's say: in the beginning was Wotan. A sky god. He didn't create the world, but he was determined to find what held the world together, and he was ambitious about gaining control over it. In our reconstructed first opera, Wotan traces the world's secret to a great ash tree, fed at the roots by a clear spring—the archetypal "tree of knowledge" and "spring of knowledge" familiar from many mythologies. Wotan asks the three Norns who spin the world's fate from the whispers of the spring if he can drink there, and is told he will have to sacrifice one of his eyes to do so. (In mythologies, there is always a price to be paid for wisdom. In some versions of Wotan's story, he hangs suspended in torment on the tree for nine days and nights.)

Wotan says he *will* give an eye to know the secret of the world. In other mythologies, Oedipus and Teiresias and Samson are all given insight when they lose their outer sight. But they lose both eyes. Wotan loses only one. His case is different. Henceforth, he will see, with his remaining eye, what he has asked to see—the world without. And he will understand it. But he will not see the world within. He will need help to understand himself.

So, with his outer-directed wisdom, interpreted for him each night by the Norns in dreams, Wotan comes to understand the natural forces that sustain

the world—earth, air, fire, and water, forces he must
bend to his will. He reaches up and breaks off a bough
from the great ash tree, and makes it into a spear. On
the weapon, which henceforth never leaves his hand,
he notches in runic script the treaties he makes with
the four elements.

With his treaties, he establishes dominion first
over his own sky people—Fricka, whom he weds,
and her brothers Donner and Froh, and her sister
Freia. He is more far-seeing than they, who know
only their own domains.

He then establishes his rule over fire. Loge, the
fire god, is hard to tame, for of his nature he pos-
sesses, not Wotan's knowledge of the workings of the
world, but quick intelligence of how to put the world
to practical purposes. But Wotan soon subdues Loge
with his spear.

By the end of our projected opera *Die Weltesche*,
Wotan has not yet bent to his will the lower elements
of water (the Rhine and his daughters) or earth (Erda),
or those lesser beings of earth, giants and humans
and dwarfs. These seem not to present much of
a problem—though, as we know, they soon shall.
Meanwhile, the world Wotan *has* subdued has reacted
against his ambition. The wound he made in the
World Ash Tree has begun to fester, and the tree to
wither, and the spring to dry up.

Who is this Wotan whose story we come so
slowly to know? Is he supposed to represent in some
way traditional notions of God? It is clear he is not a
creator, and he is by no means omnipotent, much as
he would like to be. He is not the source of life but a
powerful manifestation of it. Wotan represents not so
much some notion of God as what there is in man that

has godlike potential. Early in the writing of the text, Wagner wrote to Röckel, "Take a good look at Wotan. He resembles *us* in every way. He is the sum total of our present consciousness." Wagner's ambitious god represents man, taking that first evolutionary step towards consciousness, reaching for it, grasping it, using it for his own ends—but not understanding himself, and so having to come to terms with intelligence (Loge) and conscience (Fricka) and all-knowing intuition (Erda). They are all important to him. But none of them can give him that most important thing that the lost eye would have seen—his inner self, his Will.

If Wagner ever thought about writing something like *Die Weltesche* as his beginning, he soon thought better of it. He gives us the essential information about Wotan in installments, and withholds the whole of the World Ash story until the start of his fourth opera, *Götterdämmerung.* So, for most of the *Ring*, we think that Alberich, stealing the gold and fashioning it into a Ring and then putting a curse on it, is the source of evil in the world. Only later, when Wotan is hurrying towards his self-destruction, do we hear that, long before Alberich, Wotan performed a similar act, and paid a price for it. And thereafter, in *Das Rheingold*, he was guilty of fraud, theft, and deception. He too is a source of evil.

He thinks the Ring is what he needs. In *Die Walküre* he has begun a long-range plan to get it back for himself. He has surrounded himself with angel daughters, the Valkyries (the gatherers of the slain). They bring the greatest of fallen heroes from the battlefields of earth to his fortress, Valhalla (the hall of the slain). Those heroes now stand ready to protect him from future attack. He has also visited the earth in different shapes—as a storm cloud, a wolf, a hunter—and he has sired a race of mortals loyal to him. His earthly son is a special hero, begotten for the sole purpose of doing—his will. He has carefully seen to it that his son is completely free of all the old treaties that he is bound by. A free agent, an outlaw, this son will steal the Ring back for his father, and this time the father will incur no guilt. Wotan has prepared his son with a tough period of training in the forest, and provided a sword that knows no runes, and a sister to be his wife: disregard for all the old laws is an essential condition for this new hero's being free.

But poor Siegmund! Is he really free? Blood always tells in mythic stories. However much we love the son when, like his father, he draws his weapon from a great ash tree, we soon see that he is, also like his father, self-destructive and doomed. Siegmund can't understand why he is always at the center of trouble. It is the father's predetermined moral treaties, notched in runes on his spear, that demand that the outlaw son die; one cannot be an outlaw and escape the watchful eyes of Fricka, eager to protect the runes which secure *her* power too. Siegmund falls, and Wotan's runic spear shatters the rune-free sword. Wotan's plan for the future lies in pieces. "I am caught in my own trap," he says when he realizes this has to happen. "I am the least free of all that lives!"

Could Wotan not have seen that this would have to be? No. Wotan cannot see to his own self.

But there *is* a character who really sees into Wotan. The character for whom the second opera of the *Ring* is named, the Valkyrie daughter Brünnhilde. Fathered from the intuitive Erda, she is a special

Valkyrie, violent as the others, but also intuitive. That is why, in Act II, she stays with her father when he looks into himself. She says, in fact, that she is—his will. That when he speaks to her he speaks to himself. She exists only to do what he wants. So, when Wotan tells her that his treaties decree that Siegmund has to die, she, the embodiment of his will, knows that he really wants Siegmund to live. True to her nature, she tries to do, not what Wotan commands, but what Wotan really wants. She tries to save Siegmund. She fails, of course. The runes are fixed. Siegmund dies. And Wotan, to keep his power, has to punish her disobedience too.

The sky god then becomes a truly tragic figure. When he laid his plan for world-mastery, he didn't realize that he would come to love the erring but essentially innocent children he sired to do his work.

Wotan loves his daughter too much to destroy her completely. She will be reduced to mortal state, and put to sleep within a wall of fire, to be wakened by the only hero brave enough to pass through to her. Both father and daughter know, without articulating it, that even when she becomes a mortal she will still work his will, and that she will be wakened by Siegmund's son, who will inherit Siegmund's mission. So Wotan's plan will continue, but differently than he thought at first, and through other children.

Something of this is indicated near the end of Act III of *Die Walküre*, by a truly wonderful transformation in the music. The brutal theme of Wotan's ash-tree spear [example 17] is quite literally dismantled by Brünnhilde. She breaks its precipitous downward thrust into four questioning fragments, as she pleads for understanding and forgiveness [example 20]. And when her father understands and takes her in his arms, her new ordering of the menacing theme of the spear is transformed by Wagner's orchestra into something ineffable [example 21]. Brünnhilde has in effect taken the age-old wisdom of the world's ash tree, destroyed the curse on it, and reconstructed it. The transformation of that brutal, menacing theme is, in brief compass, what the whole of the *Ring* is about. The spear which has ruled the world with force, through treaties and compacts made with nature, will in the future be replaced by something that Wotan has begun, despite himself, to feel for his daughter—a power mightier than his spear but built from it. A transformation of his will.

In the final two parts of the *Ring*, *Siegfried* and *Götterdämmerung*, Wotan allows his Schopenhauerian world to be destroyed by his own children, in the hope that they can transform it into something new. This they eventually do, in the purification through fire and water that ends the cycle. And though Wotan is destroyed in the flames, the best part of him is transformed into a new power to rule a new world.

WELL, THE LONGER I live with the *Ring*—or, shall I say, the older and, perhaps, the wiser I get—the more I identify with Wotan. And the same was true of Wagner. As he wrote his four texts in reverse order, tracing his story back to its beginnings, he saw Wotan grow and grow in importance. Each new preface was a further explanation of his father god—his greatest tragic figure, a figure for any of us who try to deal with the unanswerable questions of life, who come finally to the realization that our vision is partial, that almost any course of action will meet with contradictions, that often our conscious plans will not, and in some cases perhaps should not, succeed. "Take a good look at Wotan," Wagner wrote. "He is us."

Wotan's most beautiful music comes at the end of this second opera, *Die Walküre*. He kisses his daughter into mortality and looks into her eyes. She has said to him, justifying her disobedience, "My eyes are yours. I only saw what you could not see." And again we wonder: Is this daughter who knows Wotan better than he knows himself—is she the vision he sacrificed when he wrested wisdom from nature? Is she, who says she is his *Wille*, the eye that sees to his inner self?

A promising new theme enters the *Ring* briefly but triumphantly in the third act of *Die Walküre*, when Sieglinde sings to the Valkyrie who has saved her, "Oh hehrstes Wunder!"—"Oh, mightiest of miracles!" [example 22]. Only recently, in newly published documents, have we discovered that Wagner thought of it as a theme for Brünnhilde. (Strange that we did not know, as Sieglinde immediately repeats the phrase to the words "Herrlichste Maid!"—"Most glorious of women!") The exultant theme will not sound again until, at the very end of the *Ring*, it comes soaring quietly over the fire and water that have destroyed Wotan's world. It will signify the transformation of Brünnhilde, Wotan's *Wille*, into what the whole of Wagner's *Ring* is striving to create—a new world. There are many wonderful moments in *Die Walküre*, which is my own favorite of the four *Ring* dramas. But there seems to me no question that the greatest single moment in the cycle comes in the closing measures of *Götterdämmerung*, when that Brünnhilde theme sounds for the last time, and signifies the transformation of Schopenhauer's pessimistic world of *Wille* into something wholly different, a new world ineffably beautiful.

At that final moment we are all likely to exclaim, as Wagner did to Liszt, "Oh, I am in a state of wonderment! Everything within me makes music. And a new world stands before me."

3

Siegfried

ACT I: *Young Siegfried, the son of Siegmund and Sieglinde, has been brought up after his mother's death by the dwarf Mime who, like his brother dwarf Alberich, has designs on the Ring. The Ring and all the treasure are still in the possession of Fafner, who has used the Tarnhelm to turn himself into a dragon, the better to guard his hoard. Mime keeps the boy Siegfried in the forest, far from any human contact, hoping that he will grow up strong enough to slay the dragon, but also stay child enough to give him the Ring when the dragon is slain. Siegfried wonders who his father and mother were, and insists that Mime reforge the sword fragments they have left him. This Mime, for all his Nibelung skills, cannot do.*

Wotan, who also has an interest in the prospective hero, visits Mime disguised once again as a mysterious stranger, "the Wanderer." Wotan challenges Mime to a game of wits with his life as forfeit, and defeats him. As Wotan leaves he tells the frightened Mime that only one who has never learned fear can forge the sword anew, and he leaves Mime's life to be claimed by whoever that fearless one might be. Mime immediately questions Siegfried and discovers that he has never learned fear, not even the fear of the forest's fire-breathing dragon. Mime knows then that young Siegfried will indeed be able to kill Fafner and get him the Ring—but that the boy might also be the one who will take his life. Siegfried, anxious to learn fear, leaps to the anvil and joyously reforges his father's sword himself, while Mime lays his plans to slay the boy after the boy has slain the dragon.

ACT II: *Deeper in the forest, Alberich and Wotan, in their first encounter since* Das Rheingold, *try to rouse the slumbering dragon-giant Fafner with warnings that he will soon lose the Ring. Mime brings Siegfried to the place and leaves him there. While the forest murmurs, Siegfried wonders again about his mother, and imitates the song of a friendly forest bird, first on a reed pipe and then on his blasting horn. The dragon wakes and attacks. Siegfried slays it in a mighty battle, and Fafner, dying, warns him that there is a curse on the gold he has guarded. The boy, tasting the dragon's blood, is suddenly able to understand the three messages the bird is singing: he must claim the golden treasure in the dragon's cave, beware of Mime who intends to kill him, and rescue a maiden who slumbers on a nearby mountain encircled by fire. Siegfried finds the Ring and Tarnhelm in the dragon's lair, slays Mime before Mime slays him, and follows the forest bird towards Brünnhilde's mountain.*

ACT III: *At the foot of that mountain, Wotan summons Erda from the earth and questions her—in vain, for she has begun to lose her powers. The sky god admits to himself the truth of what the earth goddess told him long ago: the world he has ruled will soon end. He predicts that Brünnhilde when she wakes will make a better world. But when Siegfried reaches the ascent to the mountain, Wotan, in one last effort to stop what must happen, confronts him. Siegfried, angered and uncomprehending, smashes the god's spear with the very sword the god had once given his father. Wotan vanishes on the instant, his power gone.*

Siegfried scales the height, passes through the wall of

fire, and finally learns fear at the sight of the slumbering Brünnhilde—the first woman he has ever seen. He wakes her with a kiss. She greets the sunlight, and then learns fear herself as the realization dawns that she is no longer a Valkyrie but a mortal woman and must give herself to a mortal man. Gradually the two fall in love over their reciprocal fears. They welcome the thought that they will someday die, and laugh at the impending end of the world.

THE BIRTH OF THE HERO Siegfried was solemnly foretold in the closing measures of *Die Walküre*. After the father god Wotan had encircled his slumbering Valkyrie daughter with a wall of fire, he, and then the orchestra, solemnly intoned the famous "Siegfried" theme [example 23]. Hardly any other opera has so impressive a close. Hardly any other character in opera has so impressive a moment. Wotan at that pronouncement seems truly to be a father god who sees into the future.

But he is no wiser than his slumbering daughter, Brünnhilde, who always saw more deeply into her father than he could himself. She said in *Die Walküre* that she was her father's will, and she seemed, in some strange way, to see with the eye that he had lost. She must have known, before he did, that the hero would someday come. And in fact it was she who first proclaimed Siegfried's coming, and sang his theme, when, several pages before her father's magisterial pronouncement, she sped Sieglinde to safety with the words, "You are carrying in your womb the noblest hero in the world."

To find the hero with that famous theme, Wagner moved farther and farther back in his imagination.

He wanted in this third opera of the *Ring* to conjure up primitive man in the springtime of the world. And his excitement mounted as his perception grew. He said of the human specimen that began to emerge in his verses: "I could see each throbbing of his pulses, each effort of his muscles as he moved. I saw the archetype of man himself."

Wagner now had to deal, for the first time, with a hero who wasn't, like the Dutchman or Tannhäuser or Lohengrin or the dying Siegfried, a mature man. "Young Siegfried," as the third opera was first called, would trace the hero's progress from boy to man. It would trace, in fact, the passage out of childhood. That meant that, again for the first time, Wagner would have to combine myth (which is in the main pessimistic, and reflects an adult psychology) with features of *Weltmärchen*, or fairy tales (which usually deal optimistically with the problems of childhood).

Young Siegfried may be almost full-grown as his opera begins, but emotionally he is still a child, companioned only by a dwarf, that fairytale symbol of arrested psychic growth. The lonely boy desperately needs other companionship. When he first appears he tells us he has been wandering in the forest, sounding his horn in the hope that it would call some true friend to his side. And when as if in answer a bear comes charging out of the trees, it enters his head that he could use this new companion to force the dwarf Mime to give him the knowledge he needs, and especially the sword he needs (the sword's name, Nothung, means "need"), to become a man.

Many people are shocked at young Siegfried's primitiveness, perhaps especially when, in Act I, he sics the bear on the helpless Mime. But the boy has never been taught gentler ways. He has learned just this much—that threatening Mime is the only way he can learn anything more. We ought not to censure but to pity him. He is thirsting for knowledge, hungry for love. And, though he doesn't know it, he is in mortal danger. Mime has of set purpose deprived him of all knowledge, and kept him from all human relationships. He has raised the boy for one purpose only—to slay the dragon that guards the Ring. Once that is done, Mime plans to do what he intended from the start—kill the boy, take the Ring, and rule the world.

Small wonder the boy befriends, as a child would, the animals, birds, and fishes for the little knowledge and love they can give him. Recall how T. H. White, drawing on mythic sources, had young King Arthur live with fishes, birds, and badgers, to learn from them. Recall how Walt Disney, with intuitive insight, gave Snow White a family of forest creatures for companion protectors as she waited amid the dwarfs for her awakening to maturity. Recall how Luke Skywalker learned his skills in the forest from the dwarf Yoda, and came to maturity when he discovered his true parentage.

More than anything, young Siegfried needs to know who his father and mother are. Mime, to keep him a child, insists that *he* is the boy's father and mother both. Perhaps Dr. Mime knows that a boy can become a man only when, psychologically, he has *become* his father and his mother. He certainly knows that this boy has it in him to kill the dragon: in myths, a dragon-slayer has the sign of the dragon in his eyes. Earlier, in *Die Walküre*, Hunding had seen the dragon glancing in the eyes of Siegfried's father and mother. Mime sees the same in the son: when he found the orphaned Siegfried he called him "the little dragon." In any case, it is only when Siegfried finally learns something of his true father and mother that he is able at last to spring into action, forge his own sword from the shattered pieces left by his father and saved by his mother, and begin his passage out of childhood.

Now, as is the rule with both hero-myths and fairy tales, all of this depicts psychological maturing. It is even possible to think of it as taking place within the psyche of any one of us who, like a child, listens. In our day, at Bayreuth, Wagner's grandson Wieland set Act I of *Siegfried* in the dark inside of a human brain; a century ago Wagner himself, as he darkened his auditorium, began *Siegfried* with a motif first identified as "purposeful brooding."

In the first act of *Siegfried*, as in much of the *Ring*, we are probing the human soul. Twentieth-century psychiatry, with evidence from dreams, can provide meanings for everything we see in Act I—the forest is the unconscious, the horn the impulse towards consciousness, the dwarf an obstacle to growth, the bear psychic energy summoned in need, the sword made anew from shattered pieces the assimilation of a lost father and mother, the longed-for Ring mastery over all the forces of the psyche. We may or may not find these explanations, with their all-too-sexual associations, particularly helpful. (As Freud is said to—or at least ought to—have remarked, "There are times when a cigar is only a cigar.") All the same, Wagner's orchestra keeps compelling us to ask what the images mean. "The music," says Thomas Mann in a famous essay, "seems to shoot up like a geyser from the precivilized bedrock depths of myth."

"What is it," Mann asks, "that elevates Wagner's

work so far above the intellectual level of all previous forms of musical drama?"

"Two forces have combined," he answers. "Psychology and myth."

Long before Freud and Jung discovered that psychology and myth illuminated each other, Wagner had intuited and exploited their interrelation. His contemporaries saw myth mostly as primitive science; it was man's first way of explaining the mysterious world around him. Wagner saw myth also as primitive psychology; it was man's first way of understanding the still more mysterious world deep within him.

So, on first hearing, the *Ring* seems to be about the cosmos—the elemental struggle of earth, air, fire, and water. But as we listen more it is impossible not to think that the human soul is the real landscape on which the four dramas of the *Ring* are enacted. Myth has always said as much about the psyche as about the cosmos, and—here is the astonishing thing about myth, and Wagner realizes it in this third part of the *Ring*—myth tells us that the patterns of the psyche within are identical with those of the cosmos without. When, in Act I, Wotan and Mime engage in their duel of questions, Mime asks about the three parts of the cosmos which Freud subsequently found in the psyche, and called the id, the ego, and the superego. And Wotan in turn asks the three questions most important to Siegfried's psychic growth—who are his parents? what is his sword? how are the fragmented pieces of his past to be forged anew for his future?

Wagner also introduced into the Siegfried myths a wholly new element—the folktale of the child learning fear. As we might expect, it was not so much conscious planning as intuition that was operating in

Wagner when he did this. The tale of "The One Who
Set Out to Learn Fear," familiar to him from the
Brothers Grimm, fastened on to him and wouldn't let
him go till he put it into his text. He has Mime attempt
to frighten Siegfried with the most fearful thing he can
think of—the sound and the sight of the dragon's fire
swirling through the forest. Siegfried, far from being
afraid, longs to experience that fear—he seems to
know, somehow, that the forest is symbolically his
dark unconscious, and the fire the knowledge that can
illuminate it. He sees fear as something from which he
can learn.

But then, as Wagner's omniscient orchestra describes the fire-breathing dragon, something startling
happens. "Deep down in the depths of the music,"
says Thomas Mann, "there is a shadowy hint of the
thing that will really teach him fear, a reminiscence of
the sleep-banished maiden, of whom Siegfried knows
nothing, but whom he is destined to waken." Amid
the dragon music we hear the motif of Brünnhilde's
slumber [example 24].

Wagner here anticipates what contemporary
writers on the psychology of myth have since
discovered—that the myth of the hero (Oedipus or
King Arthur or Siegfried) describes the psychological
maturing of the adolescent male, and that devouring
monsters in the hero-myth represent something pre-
cisely identifiable in the male psyche, namely the
frightening aspect of the feminine. The "anima," as
Jung called the male's inner feminine, is potentially
destructive, potentially creative; the maturing male
must defeat its dangerous side and release its creative
power. (So the medieval knight, when he finds his
sword and slays his dragon, frees a maiden, and

marries her.) Wagner saw the psychological truth of this long before we did, and hid the theme of the slumbering feminine deep within his fear-inducing dragon music.

No scene in the *Ring* is richer in these interpenetrations of music, myth, and psychology than the Forest Murmurs we spoke about in chapter one. Siegfried lies alone beneath forest trees which allow only intermittent shafts of morning light to appear, waiting for the moment when, with his horn, he can summon up the next "companion" to contribute to his maturing—the dragon. Just as modern psychology would have it, his thoughts turn to the feminine, to the mother he has never known. Subtly, gradually, the music re-creates, in this leafy enclosure, the feminine, watery world in which the *Ring* began. The murmuring of the *Siegfried* trees sounds like the rippling of the *Rheingold* waves. The cry of the *Siegfried* forest echoes the cry of the water creatures in *Rheingold*. And the forest bird in *Siegfried* intones almost note for note the Rhine maidens' song "Weia, Waga"—"Wander, you wave, waft to the cradle."

The scene at the *Ring*'s beginning is a cradle song for the new world evolving. And the return of those feminine motifs at this midpoint in the *Ring* implies that the world, once alive with pristine innocence, now has a hero, Siegfried, who can make it new again. "The purpose of a hero," Hegel said, "is to bring a new world into existence."

There are other Freudian elements in the Forest Murmurs scene. Thomas Mann finds "a presentient complex of mother-fixation, sexual desire, and Angst." And there is a fairytale element, too—in the bird that appears as if in answer to Siegfried's mother-longings. A little-known episode in the Cinderella story, reported by Bruno Bettelheim in *The Uses of Enchantment*, tells how Cinderella asked her father, not for beautiful clothes or jewels, as her stepsisters did, but only for "the first twig that presses against your hat." This she planted on her mother's grave, and watered with her tears. It grew to be a wondrous tree where three times a day a white bird would meet her and tell what she needed to know. The mother's wisdom thus passed, with the father's assistance, into the child. Similarly in Wagner's opera the forest bird appears to Siegfried when he wonders about his mother, and eventually speaks to him three times (triple groupings are a feature of fairy tales), telling him what he needs to know. He is able to understand the bird after he has tasted the dragon's blood—that is to say, when he has defeated the destructive aspect of the feminine anima and released its creative potential.

Then, in Act III, comes the young hero's encounter with Wotan—a scene chock full of mythic images to conjure with. The mother's bird (intuition) flees before the father god's two ravens (called Reason and Memory in the old Eddas Wagner used). Wotan wears his hat across his face as he goes against the wind. He sees the eye he forfeited long ago now staring back at him from the boy's face. He knows that the treaties he has made with nature and notched on his spear have not ruled the world rightly. He holds that spear aloft so that the sword it once shattered may now, reforged by the son of his son, smash it in turn. Like the myths where Oedipus and Jason and Perseus encounter and defeat "the father," the scene between Siegfried and Wotan depicts the young male's assertion of independence as he moves past the father of his father to find himself.

Or, more technically, his Self.

Wagner's young hero discovers his Self within *Siegfried*'s most famous and suggestive symbol—the circle of fire around the slumbering Brünnhilde. That flaming barrier is there to symbolize the fear which he must experience in order to love, and the illumination which love will bring him. It means something too for the heroine—the final scene of *Siegfried* at last gives us something of the psychology of the maturing female. The wall of fire is there to protect her (as the wall of thorns protects Sleeping Beauty) from sexual awakening before she is ready for it.

As he passes through the encompassing fire, Siegfried once again sounds his horn to summon up a companion, and at last his longing for love is fulfilled, for at last he finds a companion to teach him fear. His frightened shout ("This is no man!" as he removes her warrior breastplate) is as psychologically right as her awaking, at his kiss, to greet, not him alone, but all the world: the response to love is life's complete answer to the child's wondering what the world means.

The "love duet" that follows is surely the strangest of all love duets in opera. It completes, triumphantly, a pattern, a maturing process in *Siegfried* that is also found in modern psychology. Carl Jung tells us that the male achieves wholeness only when he has faced three archetypal forces—the shadow, the anima, and the Wise Old Man—and then integrated these experiences in some circular, centripetal pattern which symbolizes his Self. In the course of *Siegfried*, the hero encounters, in correct Jungian order, Mime (the shadow), the dragon (the anima), Wotan (the Wise Old Man), and—in the circle of fire—Brünnhilde, who tells him, astonishingly, "I am your Self."

Siegfried learns other astonishing things about the woman he wakens. She is not, as he first thinks, his mother, but there is something of his mother in her: the orchestra tells us he sees the dragon in her eyes. And she has a role to play, not just in his maturing, but in the world to which she awakes: like the virgin Athene pre-existing in the mind of Zeus, like Holy Wisdom in the Book of Proverbs, assisting the Creator at the making of the world, Brünnhilde knew the father god's will long ago. And it will be her role now to fulfill that will as the old world ends and a new world rises.

In the duet Brünnhilde too, for the first time, learns fear. She is now a mortal woman, trembling on the brink of surrender to human love. When her fear is at its height, Wagner writes in his manuscript, "a beautiful idea occurs to her." He has his orchestra intone the familiar melody of his separately composed "Siegfried Idyll," while his text indicates that the "beautiful idea" is the Romantic notion, first stated by Goethe and always evolving in Wagner's mind, that the *Ewig-Weibliche*, the "eternal feminine," will lead the aspiring masculine onward. As the duet hurries to its end, Brünnhilde's imagery, streaming throughout the text, is the feminine symbol, water; Siegfried's is masculine fire. And, very strangely for a "love duet," the two lovers foresee the impending destruction of the old world through fire and water, and they laugh with joy. They seem to know that it will be through fire and water that the world will be transformed at the end of the *Ring*, and that it is they who will accomplish that transformation.

Each of them, we now know, sees with the lost eye of Wotan. Each is an embodiment of his will. It is now Wotan's will that the world of *Wille* be destroyed and transformed into something newer and purer.

SIEGFRIED IS a pioneer's journey into areas drama had never before attempted, and psychology was only beginning to become aware of. Pioneering efforts are never completely successful. Early in the composition of *Siegfried*, Wagner wrote, "I am convinced that this will be my most popular work. It will make its way quickly and joyously and will pull the other pieces along, one by one, so that it will likely be the founder of a whole Nibelungen dynasty."

That has not proved to be the case. In many theaters, *Siegfried* is the least often performed of the four *Ring* operas, possibly the least performed of Wagner's ten major works.

Reasons for this are not hard to seek. Long stretches of dialogue in Acts I and II fall in musical invention below the level of anything in the other parts of the cycle. More than two hours elapse before we hear a single female voice, and then we hear only an occasional chirp from the forest bird. The title role calls for an energetic youth with the vocal equipment of a forty-year-old Heldentenor, requires him to sing for hours over an often tumultuous orchestra, and then tests his exhausted voice against the radiant high Cs of a well-rested soprano. Alberich, when at last he re-appears, seems to have lost, not just the Ring, but most of his dramatic stature. And Mime can be seen, all too fatally, as an anti-Semitic caricature—Mahler certainly saw him as such. And though Mahler in his day didn't take offense, Mime's death at the proto-German hero's hands is, for many in our day, the *Ring*'s most distasteful moment.

But perhaps the main reason for *Siegfried*'s relative unpopularity is the startling newness, the perception, the daring at work as Wagner explores myth for its psychological insights. Some failure is, in so ambitious an undertaking, only to be expected. Wagner abandoned the *Ring* for a while, once he got his Siegfried under those forest trees in Act II. Then, when he'd finished Act II, he abandoned the *Ring* for almost twelve years, and turned to writing *Tristan* and *Die Meistersinger.* There were practical reasons for his doing this, but he likely felt as well that he lacked something of the naiveté essential to telling *Siegfried*'s fairytale story. And perhaps he felt too that the *Ring* was becoming something even he couldn't understand.

All that said, *Siegfried* is a wonderful opera. It has, of the four *Ring* dramas, possibly the most delicate orchestral details (in the Forest Murmurs), the most important of the great confrontation scenes (the face-off between Wotan and Siegfried), and the most rapturous single passage (Brünnhilde's awakening). And as the *Ring* continues to be performed with increasing frequency all over the world, our appreciation of *Siegfried* will surely grow. I don't think we've taken the full measure of it yet. We need to hear it more.

Bruno Bettelheim, in his book on fairy tales, tells us why children ask to hear the same stories over and over, in the dark, with their imaginations alerted: only by degrees can they absorb the wisdom the tales have to give. We too are coming by degrees to see what wisdom lies in the *Ring*. Wagner himself only gradually came to see that his intuitive musical myth was describing, not a social and political, but a psychological and metaphysical reality. It was asking: who am I? where did I come from? what is the meaning of life? what is the world? Those are not the revolutionary's questions, or the politician's. They are the philosopher's questions. And also the child's.

That, surely, is one reason why the myth-maker of Bayreuth was the first of all composers to darken his theater as he told his stories.

4
Götterdämmerung

PROLOGUE: *The three Norns, spinning the threads of past, present, and future atop Brünnhilde's mountain, tell how Wotan long ago gained control over the world when he drank at the stream of wisdom and broke off a branch of the world ash tree, making it his spear, and inscribing on it his covenant with nature. Now the spear has been shattered, the spring has dried up, the ash tree has withered, and Wotan has ordered his slain heroes to pile its timbers around Valhalla. Soon he will thrust the broken end of his spear into Loge's breast, and fire will issue forth to consume the world. Of what will happen after that the Norns can see nothing— only a dim vision of Alberich and his Ring. Their thread breaks in their hands, and they descend to their mother, Erda. The world's seers have lost their power.*

Day dawns, and the hope for the future, Siegfried and Brünnhilde, declare their love as he sets out on further adventures. He gives her the golden Ring that he won as a boy and she gives him Grane, the heroic steed that she rode as a young Valkyrie. He descends to the Rhine and journeys upstream.

ACT I: *In a castle on the Rhine, the villainous Hagen tells his cowardly half-brother, the Gibichung king Gunther, that he should take Brünnhilde to wife, and that his sister Gutrune would find a wealthy husband in Siegfried. Hagen himself is mainly interested in getting Siegfried's Ring. The three of* them give *Siegfried*, on his arrival, *a potion that makes him forget Brünnhilde and fall in love with Gutrune*. Gunther then asks Siegfried, after they have ceremoniously become blood brothers, to *win Brünnhilde for him*. Siegfried, as one last fleeting vision of the past dies in his memory, agrees to scale the mountain, pass through the fire, and subdue Brünnhilde—while disguised, through the Tarnhelm's magic, as Gunther. The duped hero and the anxious suitor head upstream together, and Hagen, hoping eventually to lord it over both of them, keeps watch on the Rhine.

On the mountaintop, *Brünnhilde* is visited by one of her Valkyrie sisters, *Waltraute, who pleads with her to give up the Ring*: their father, *Wotan*, sits in state surrounded by his warrior guardsmen, *awaiting the end of his world*. Only once did his grim visage soften—when he thought of Brünnhilde. The *world will end unless the Ring is restored to its natural owners, the Rhine maidens*. Brünnhilde refuses to part with the Ring; it is Siegfried's token of love. Waltraute rides off in despair. Then, in terrible irony, the very *Siegfried who had given Brünnhilde the Ring suddenly appears, wrests the Ring from her finger, and claims her for Gunther*. She thinks that he, wearing the Tarnhelm, really is Gunther. For honor's sake, Siegfried places the sword Nothung *between himself and Brünnhilde* that night.

ACT II: *Hagen* is visited in his sleep by his *father*, and we understand how he came to know so much about Siegfried, and to have such a special interest in the Ring: his father is *Alberich*. Hagen is the one Wotan knew would come, the Nibelung's son sired for the sole purpose of recovering the Nibelung's Ring. Alberich reminds his son in the night that Siegfried, who now wears the Ring, must be destroyed.

At dawn *Siegfried* re-appears at the castle, magically transported from Brünnhilde's mountain by the Tarnhelm, *announcing that Gunther will follow soon with his new bride, Brünnhilde. Hagen summons the Gibichung vassals, more loyal to him than to King Gunther, who now arrives with the captive Brünnhilde. She is astonished to see Siegfried in this dreadful company, and suspects the worst when she sees the Ring on his finger. Hearing that he is to marry Gutrune, she swears an oath that he has lain with her. He, knowing nothing of the past, swears that he has not, and leaves to prepare for his wedding. Hagen offers to right the wrong, to kill Siegfried, and the humiliated Brünnhilde reveals that the hero's only vulnerable spot, unprotected by her magic spells, is his back. Gunther, thinking that Siegfried took advantage of his Tarnhelm disguise to lie with Brünnhilde, joins in the conspiracy against him, even while the wedding procession forms.*

ACT III: During a hunt on the wooded banks of the Rhine, the three water nymphs invite Siegfried to amorous dalliance, but he remains faithful to the only wife he remembers, Gutrune. They then tell him that the Ring he wears is cursed, and almost persuade him to give it to them, but he keeps it to prove his fearlessness. They predict that he will soon die, and swim away to find Brünnhilde, but not before Hagen and his fellow hunters have served Siegfried an antidote to the potion, so that he remembers his past again. Just when he has traced his way through memory to the moment when he awakened Brünnhilde, Hagen stabs him in the back. Wotan's ravens, who have watched for good tidings or ill, fly up to tell their god it is time for his world to end. Siegfried dies remembering Brünnhilde as she greeted him on her awakening.

Siegfried's body is borne in sorrow to the Gibichung castle. Gutrune in tears accuses Gunther of murder, but the exultant Hagen insists that the credit for the slaying is his:

Siegfried is his spoil from the hunt. Hagen then kills Gunther in a quarrel over the Ring, and reaches to take the cursed thing from Siegfried's finger, only to shrink back when the dead arm rises to threaten him. Everyone retreats as Brünnhilde takes command of the hall. She has learned the whole truth of the Gibichungs' treachery from the Rhine maidens, and now orders that a funeral pyre be raised for Siegfried's body. Solemnly she tells Wotan, ready for the end in Valhalla, that he can fade away at last. Then she takes the Ring from Siegfried's finger, puts his body to the torch, and rides Grane into the flames to die with her beloved.

The world is then purified through water (the Rhine floods the castle and the Rhine maidens rise to take the Ring from Brünnhilde) and fire (Valhalla too has been set ablaze and can be seen flaming in the sky). Hagen sinks to his death in the Rhine, drawn by the water nymphs to the depths where his father began the whole cycle. The music indicates that a new world is rising, a world that, if we read the Ring right, Wotan has finally willed into being through his wonderful daughter Brünnhilde.

GÖTTERDÄMMERUNG. What does it mean—this twilight of the gods, this dusking, disappearing, fading away of the gods? Wotan *dies* in this opera, his world ash tree in flaming pieces. What does it mean when a god dies?

Something of an answer to that awesome question begins on Pentecost Sunday, 1869, as a young professor of classics walks around the Lake of Lucerne to Tribschen, the house picturesquely set below the mountaintop where, legend has it, Pontius Pilate lies buried, and a perennial cloud tells us he still weeps for the time he sentenced a God to die.

The young professor stands at the gate for a long time, listening and wondering as he hears from within a chord struck over and over again on the piano. Wagner is inside that house, waiting out another Swiss exile, composing *Siegfried*. Eventually the twenty-four-year-old fledgling classicist screws up his courage, rings the bell, and receives an invitation to return to lunch the next day. Thereafter, he spends many long days in conversation with Lucerne's resident genius, the composer of the *Ring*.

Wagner, plagued as always with self-doubts, is delighted to have found a brilliant young intellectual who admires his work. And Nietzsche, for that is the young classicist's name, thinks that in Wagner he has found Aeschylus come alive again.

As it turned out, not even Wagner—strong-willed, intuitive, neo-pagan though he was—could live up to Friedrich Nietzsche's superhuman ideals. There was bound to be some disillusionment on both sides, and there was. But before the famous break-up, Nietzsche wrote a book more important for understanding Greek tragedy than any since Aristotle twenty-four centuries earlier. That book, *The Birth of Tragedy from the Spirit of Music*, Nietzsche had talked through with Wagner.

And later, in Nietzsche's most famous work, one that has sent intellectual shock waves across the philosophies of our century, a mythical prophet named Zarathustra descends from his mountains to announce, not in exultation but in sorrow, "God is dead." The Age of Reason, Nietzsche says, has killed the father god whom mankind needed and loved. Now, with the Age of Reason also discredited, mankind must be made to face the abyss—the nothingness—that remains. Only then can it find, *within itself*, the new creative force that will sustain it in a world without God.

That was not the first time that the death of God had been proclaimed in a great work of literature. Twenty-five centuries previous, in the central chorus of his *Agamemnon*, Aeschylus sang that, long before the god he worshipped, two previous dynasties of gods had risen and fallen. There had been two older father gods who had ruled the world, and passed away.

What does it all mean? We may account for the rise and fall of the Greek father gods in this way. Primitive man, dimly conscious of earth and sea, sun and moon, worshipped them as cosmic gods, under the dominion of father sky, Uranos. Then, over the eons, threatened by thunderstorms, earthquakes, volcanos, and tidal waves, man, still brutish but more aware, came to think of Uranos as overthrown when his violent son Kronos, with his Titans, took over the world. Finally, as man learned to think and to feel, and became fully conscious of himself and his own powers, Kronos was thought to have been dethroned by *his* son Zeus, a god of consciousness, with a sophisticated dynasty of Olympian gods representing, not just sky and sea, thunderstorm and rainbow, but also thought and love, domesticity and creativity. But the Zeus of myth knows that a time will come when he too will pass away, and he fears it.

The question in all of this then becomes: Does god die, or is it rather that evolving man emerges into new levels of awareness and so, feeling the changes in himself, changes his god?

It was a question asked in Wagner's time by

Ludwig Feuerbach, and answered by him emphatically: what we call God is actually man's projection of his inner self.

Wagner was profoundly influenced by that idea, and also by the early German Romanticists, Novalis and Schelling and the two Schlegels and Herder, and their approach to myth, so widely accepted today— that man's myths are the repositories of eternal truths about himself. Friedrich Schlegel saw the spirit that sustained the world and irradiated every human soul as love. (So the trouble in the world of Wagner's *Ring* begins when the original sinner renounces love, and it ends with an affirmation, in the music, of healing love.) German philosophers in the nineteenth century were also concerned with opposites, antinomies, in mutual contradiction; for Kant, conscious reason led to contradictions, and only a "categorical imperative" —intuitive knowledge of the moral law—could reconcile them. (So in the *Ring* Wotan finds himself trapped by the contradictions of his various rational plans, and only his inner knowledge, Brünnhilde, sees through to their resolution.) For Hegel and Marx, the collision of those contradictions "thesis" and "antithesis" is necessary for the achievement of any synthesis. (So in this concluding opera Siegfried and Brünnhilde must be set on a collision course which destroys them both, but brings about the final synthesis.)

In short, while Wagner was shaping his four dramas, he was attuned to the philosophic ideas that were shaping his Europe. He thought at the start that his *Ring* would be an image of his century's politics. But, as we've observed, he gradually saw it turn from political to metaphysical concerns. At the end of the *Ring*, man rises to a new level of awareness. It is as if he has seen the third god, Zeus (or Wotan, or whatever we choose to call the god of consciousness), pass away, just as the previous gods had done. And a new force appears to rule the world.

Who or what is that new power? That is what *Götterdämmerung* is about.

I'VE SPOKEN at some length, in these chapters, of Wotan and Siegfried and Brünnhilde. But I've hardly mentioned the important figure who began the *Ring*'s story and returns vividly in Act II of *Götterdämmerung*. Alberich. In some ways, this Nibelung dwarf is the main character in the *Ring*. In fact the whole cycle is called *The Ring of the Nibelung*—that is to say, *The Ring of Alberich*, or, if you want to translate the word "Nibelung," *The Ring of the One Who Dwells in Mist*. Alberich the mist-dweller appears in three of the four operas, and at the central moment in the opera in which he does not appear, *Die Walküre*, Wotan remembers him in whispers and dread. He is clearly important. At the end of the cycle, when all the other main characters are gone, he survives. The three Rhine maidens have their gold again, and possibly the whole cycle can start over. If Alberich comes back. Will he? Wagner's title, *Der Ring des Nibelungen*, could also mean "the endless cycle the Nibelung begins." It's hard to get rid of Alberich.

The cosmic struggle in the *Ring* is between Alberich and Wotan. The sky god even calls himself and the dwarf Light-Alberich and Dark-Alberich, perhaps indicating thereby that he and the Nibelung are opposed manifestations of the same force. Each is bent on world power, and needs the Ring to get it. Each fathers a son to get him the Ring. But there is a difference between them. Wotan and his son and his son's son all die. Alberich's son, Hagen, goes in the end to a watery grave. But Alberich himself—we remember only after Wagner's last suspended chord has died away—Alberich still lives!

And yet, we think, what power can he have? In order to steal the gold in the first place, Alberich had to renounce love. And when he cursed the Ring fashioned from the gold, that lovelessness spread over all the world. The whole terrible story—the loveless betrayals and deaths of those who wear the Ring, and the vengeful and savage acts of those who covet it—all of that is the inevitable working out of Alberich's curse. But in the end, when the Ring becomes natural gold again in the waves, the one thing that can defeat Alberich comes sounding across the water and through the fire—what Sieglinde called, when she first sang the phrase [example 22] in *Die Walküre*, "the mightiest of miracles." With that force to replace the dying god Wotan, can Alberich really begin the cycle anew? No, Alberich will *not* be the new god to rule the world. For at the end of the *Ring* we have, not a return to the beginning, but a transformation.

If the end of the *Ring* were a return to the beginning, Wagner would have brought his music back to its original key, E flat. But just when we feel the tonality turn, on the last page, towards E flat, the music shifts, and shifts, and shifts, through a series of awe-inspiring chord progressions. And we end in a new key, D flat, with that "mightiest of miracles" theme, which seems to look, not back, but forward, to a new beginning.

Not all of *Götterdämmerung* is concerned with such cosmic matters. Some of it is rather ordinary melodrama. Wagner, now at the height of his musical powers, has come at last to setting to music the story of the dastardly Burgundian family he crafted out of the medieval *Nibelungenlied* a quarter of a century before, and the old plot is not always equal to the new music, or to the philosophies Wagner has since waded through. Bernard Shaw certainly thought as much, and Wagner too came to have doubts about the story he started with years before—Siegfried's death. Eventually he confided to his second wife, Cosima, that he no longer thought of Siegfried as a tragic figure to set beside others in the *Ring*. Siegfried seems to have got lost in the shuffle when his myths were conflated with the myth of the twilight of the gods, when Wotan and Alberich and Brünnhilde began to gain in importance, and the *Ring* to wonder about not just the hero, but the cosmos.

But from the death of Siegfried, with its stupendous funeral march, to the closing page, *Götterdämmerung* rises to a level many will say is unsurpassed in any work for the stage. And the part that Siegfried plays in this is surprising. It had been Wagner's first intention, twenty-five years previous, to have Brünnhilde take Siegfried after his death to a heroic afterlife with Wotan in Valhalla. But Wagner changed the text of that final scene—five times. He introduced the world-destruction myth, the old Norse Ragnarok, and that tremendous finale, Brünnhilde's immolation. In the fourth version, he had Brünnhilde speak like Feuerbach, in the fifth like Schopenhauer. But in the sixth and final version, he cut most of his text and let the music explain that Siegfried's innocent death gives

Brünnhilde the insight that enables her, who still is Wotan's will, to do what she knows Wotan wants her to do—transform his old world into a new world.

So the last two themes we hear are those associated with the hero and heroine who possess Wotan's lost vision, and embody his will—Siegfried [example 23] and Brünnhilde [example 22]. In the end, Wagner, sensing that his *Ring* was as much about the human psyche as about the whole world, let his music say what, years before, he had written to his friend Röckel: "Siegfried alone is not the complete human person. He is only the half. It is only with Brünnhilde that Siegfried transforms the world." Wagner was still concerned with that, writing an essay on the feminine element in human nature, the day he died.

Now I must say at length what I have meant from the first to say. The *Ring* can be thought of as taking place, not only in its natural landscape of rivers and mountains covered by fir trees (the way Wagner wanted it on the stage), and not only in a nineteenth-century industrialized Europe endangered by greed and corrupting materialism (the way Wagner first thought of it, and some modern productions stage it), but in that inner landscape which is Wagner's and mine and yours (the way Wagner eventually suggested we see it).

On that inner level, Wotan and Alberich, Siegfried and Brünnhilde are four inner impulses, four aspects of consciousness—the present state of human evolution. Consciousness as light and dark, as male and female. You may want to add Fricka as conscience, and Loge as intelligence, and Erda as intuition, and those other characters, especially the human characters, as the sorrows and desires and fears that inhabit your inner landscape.

That will make Wagner's *Ring* fit what Schlegel and the other German Romantics were saying, that the myths of the gods were about man, that the secret of the universe lay in each human soul. It will explain why Fricka knows what Wotan tries to hide, why Erda knows what Wotan must do, why Loge knows how to implement what Wotan plans: that is the way conscience and intuition and intelligence work for consciousness.

Seen this way, the *Ring* is a story of a soul in crisis. The great elemental world of gods and men is also the private world of man's inner struggle with his own destructive impulses, of his awareness of limitations and guilt, of the emergence in him of new ideas, and the dying in him of transforming deaths.

Wagner once said something very startling about his *Ring*. He said that it teaches us that "we must learn to die." We must "will what is necessary and bring it to pass." The great deaths in myths are symbols of inner transformations in man, who makes the myths. In this myth, Wotan—the god of consciousness—dies. Wagner didn't originally intend that. He intended that Erda, when she appears in *Das Rheingold*, would warn Wotan that his power would end *unless* he gave up the Ring. Later, he revised Erda's warning to read, "All that exists ends. A dark day is dawning for the gods. I counsel you—give up the Ring." Relinquishing its power is not an alternative. Wotan will pass away in any case. He must accept the loss of his power, and embrace his death.

At the end of the *Ring*, the god of consciousness dies. And his voluntary withdrawal leaves the world

within us to be ruled henceforth, not by the consciousness he represents, but by that "mightiest of miracles"
[example 22], the transformation wrought by his
daughter Brünnhilde. The *Ring*, which began as a
parable of Europe's evolution towards a classless,
progressive society, eventually—to Wagner's sur-
prise, and after many revisions—became a parable of
a god's voluntary death, and the transformation that
results. It is indeed about evolution, but it is as far in
advance of Darwin's theory (developed at almost
exactly the same time) as myth has always been in
advance of science. It begins with a god newly established in power and ends with that god consumed in
flames. That is to say, it begins with the emergence of
man into consciousness, and ends with consciousness
voluntarily yielding to—*the next evolutionary development in human nature.*

That, I suggest, is why Wagner couldn't put the
end of the *Ring* into words, even in six separate
attempts. As he labored over his mythic cycle, an
intuitive idea kept hammering away at him, year after
year—perhaps the most important idea of his century,
and not to be fulfilled for centuries to come, though
man's myths knew, and had always known, it would
someday happen: *man was meant to evolve beyond his
present state*, even as he had evolved into it. But this
step would require the death of his present consciousness, and its transformation into—Wagner could only
say what that was in music, in the theme to which
Sieglinde once sang the words "mightiest of miracles," the theme associated with the transformation of
Wotan's will, Brünnhilde.

NOW PERHAPS I can align the *Ring* with an evolutionary parable of our own century. A parable millions of
young people responded to, though they couldn't say
why. A parable introduced by the music Richard
Strauss wrote for Nietzsche's Zarathustra. In that
marvelous film, *2001*, Stanley Kubrick shows (in his
prologue) the evolution of ape to conscious man and
(in his epilogue) the evolution of man to his next
stage, completed when he lands his spaceship on
Jupiter. There is a computer brain on the ship, the sum
total of man's present intelligence. The computer tries
to prevent man's further evolution, for that would
mean the end of its power. The lone surviving astro-
naut realizes that the computer must be destroyed. He
defuses it, function by function. And when its last two
functions—reason and memory—are defused, man
lands on his new planet and evolves to his new stage.
He is transformed.

That intuitive film is very close to *Götterdämmerung*. In the old prose Edda that Wagner used as
one of his sources, Wotan's two ravens are called
Reason and Memory. In *Götterdämmerung*, Wotan
sends them off to witness Siegfried's death. Then they
fly back to die with their god, whom Wagner called
"the sum of our present awareness." And the world is
transformed.

If this view of the *Ring* as evolutionary is correct,
we have some explanation of why young C. S. Lewis
responded to it as he did, and you and I may have on
our first experience of it, especially if we came to the
Ring when we were very young. The *Ring* is about us.
About our unarticulated dreams and aspirations.
About an evolutionary potential in us we sense only at
moments of heightened awareness. At the end of

the *Ring*, it is as if a door has opened, as if the sky
has turned round, as if, in the words of C. S.
Lewis remembering his childhood, we have "tasted
heaven": Yes, that is I. That is the center of my feeling
and awareness. That expresses a longing in me I
hardly know I have.

Wagner's mythic *Ring* tells us what we are. We
are the world in which Wotan confronts Alberich and
Brünnhilde and Siegfried, and Fricka and Erda and
Loge. Each of us is a world flawed and fallible
and destined to die, full of destructive impulses, yet
capable too of goodness and heroism, open to beauty
and joy, and destined for greater things than we
know. Like all great art, and in concert with the great
religions of the world, the *Ring* assures us that our
lives have meaning—even, perhaps especially, the
sorrows and the pain and the deaths in them, for
those are transforming experiences. And though our
consciousness is, like Wotan himself, finite, we sense
that we are meant to move towards something beyond consciousness that is infinite. That comes rush-
ing in on us on a wave of sound as the *Ring* reaches its
last page.

EVERY COMMENTATOR on the *Ring* must end by saying
this: no single interpretation of the work encompasses
it all. Not Shaw's, not Donington's, not Cooke's,
certainly not mine, and—I must say this too, for he
has been my authority at every turn—not even Wagner's. Artists from Plato to the present have freely
admitted that the artist himself does not fully understand his own creation. "How can he hope to have his
intuitive perceptions understood by others," Wagner

wrote, "when he himself stands before an enigma, and can suffer the same illusions as anyone else?"

Because the scope of the *Ring* is not much less than the world itself, no single interpretation will do. But try to understand it we must. Wagner himself used it to seek self-understanding. And he seems at last to have understood that the immense world his music creates and transforms in the *Ring* is the outer world of nature and, even more, the inner world of the human soul.

Further Reading

Books and articles on Wagner are said to outnumber those on any other person known to history save only Jesus and, possibly, Napoleon. Here are fifteen of the more than twenty-two thousand publications on the composer of the Ring, *selected for the range and depth of their analyses and their pertinence to the present volume. Most of these studies were first published in Britain; I have listed their American publishers for the convenience of the majority of those who will read this book.*

Burbidge, Peter, and Sutton, Richard, eds., *The Wagner Companion* (New York: Cambridge University Press, 1979). A remarkable collection of essays by a galaxy of Wagner scholars. Contains the brilliant and controversial piece "The Total Work of Art," by Michael Tanner (Wagner is life-affirming, and his works are a succession of related truths that make sense of the world); "Wagner's Musical Language" by Deryck Cooke (Wagner's music is, consistently from work to work, bound to the contents of the unconscious); and Lucy Beckett's "Wagner and his Critics," a humanistic overview of what Wagner meant to Berlioz, Baudelaire, Mallarmé, Lawrence, Joyce, Eliot, Nietzsche, and Mann (Wagner's achievement is both intellectual and intuitive and "those who guess that they have something to learn from it are right").

Cooke, Deryck, *I Saw the World End: A Study of Wagner's Ring* (New York: Oxford University Press, 1979). A masterly study that was brought to a halt by its author's untimely death not quite halfway through his proposed plan. The opening sections boldly point out the limitations of Newman (who nonetheless blazed the trail), Donington (whom Cooke helped to some of his best insights), and Shaw (who is not quite so easy a target as he might seem). What follows is impressive enough to suggest that this might have been the best analysis of the *Ring* ever written in any language. Characteristically brilliant is Cooke's demonstration that Freia is, first and foremost, the goddess of love, and that her entrance theme, long misnamed "Flight," is actually Wagner's basic love motif, from *Lohengrin* through the *Ring* to *Tristan* and *Die Meistersinger*.

Dahlhaus, Carl, *Richard Wagner's Music Dramas*, trans. Mary Whittall (New York: Cambridge University Press, 1979, originally published in 1971). Succinct, closely argued, demanding, sometimes excessively schematic essays on Wagner's ten major works. Though he is no uncritical disciple, Dahlhaus all but convinces any of the hitherto unconvinced that Wagner's interacting text and music raise drama to a degree of expressiveness beyond the reach of any other dramatist of the sung or spoken word.

Deathridge, John, and Dahlhaus, Carl, *The New Grove Wagner* (New York: W. W. Norton, 1984). Such is the accelerating pace of Wagner studies that in four years the Wagner entry in *The New Grove Dictionary of Music and Musicians* was in need of wholesale overhaul. Here Deathridge and Dahlhaus take over from the earlier Curt von Westernhagen, and many commonplaces of Wagner criticism, as well as many misrepresentations perpetrated by Wagner himself in his autobiography, *Mein Leben*, bite the dust. The reader begins to feel (and he just may be right) that only now are we beginning to understand the complex phenomenon Wagner is.

Donington, Robert, *Wagner's "Ring" and Its Symbols: The Music and the Myth*, 3rd ed. (New York: Faber and Faber, 1974, originally published in 1963). The now-famous study of the *Ring* in terms of Jungian depth psychology and Joseph Campbell's reading of myth. The analysis presupposes an ability to read music (and reading Donington it is as if one reads the music for the first time), but it does not presuppose any special knowledge of Jung—psychological concepts are explained for the uninitiated as they arise in the argument. An astonishing tour de force that has influenced both the criticism and the staging of the *Ring*.

Gregor-Dellin, Martin, *Richard Wagner: His Life, His Work, His Century*, trans. J. Maxwell Brownjohn (San Diego: Harcourt Brace Jovanovich, 1983). The best one-volume biography available in English, scholarly, fair-minded, and readable, but in a translation unconsciously abridged from the original German.

Lloyd-Jones, Hugh, *Blood for the Ghosts: Classical Influences in the Nineteenth and Twentieth Centuries* (Baltimore: Johns Hopkins Press, 1983). Contains the pioneering essay "Wagner and the Greeks" from *The Times Literary Supplement* of January 9, 1976.

Magee, Bryan, *Aspects of Wagner*, 2nd ed. (New York: Oxford University Press, 1988, originally published in 1968). After two decades still the best short introduction to

Wagner. Five pointed essays on perhaps the five most controversial aspects of the composer—his aesthetics, his anti-Semitism, his cult, his influence, and the special difficulties involved in performing his music. The writing is so clear and clean that Wagner's tortured arguments become intelligible almost for the first time. Updated in 1988 with a less-than-compelling chapter on the special importance of music among the other constituents of the *Gesamtkunstwerk*.

Mann, Thomas, *Pro and Contra Wagner*, tr. Allan Blunden (Chicago: University of Chicago Press, 1985). In a series of letters and occasional pieces, the great novelist never quite makes up his mind about the ambivalent composer to whom he owes so much. This volume contains new translations of the lecture "The Sorrows and Grandeur of Richard Wagner," written in 1933 and still one of the most penetrating pieces ever written on Wagner, and the almost equally remarkable "Richard Wagner and *Der Ring des Nibelungen*," written in 1937.

Millington, Barry, *Wagner* (New York: Vintage, 1987, originally published in 1984). The best one-volume analysis of Wagner's life and work, both sensitive and sensible, with the up-to-date details one now misses in Ernest Newman's four volumes.

Newman, Ernest, *The Life of Richard Wagner*, four volumes (New York: Cambridge University Press, 1976, originally published 1933–47). The classic biography, one of the great works of musical scholarship, but lacking the revelations provided by such recently released primary biographical sources as Cosima's diaries and Wagner's own notebook, *The Brown Book*.

————, *The Wagner Operas* (New York: Alfred A. Knopf, 1981, originally published as *Wagner Nights*, 1949). Long the standard volume for plot synopses cum musical examples and background detail. Any Wagnerite in good standing knows it by heart.

Rather, L. J., *The Dream of Self-Destruction: Wagner's Ring and the Modern World* (Baton Rouge: Louisiana State University Press, 1979). A professor emeritus of medicine at Stanford, author of *The Genesis of Cancer: A Study of the History of Ideas*, offers a guided tour through some of the most infested Wagnerian quagmires—the nineteenth-century myth of Nordic supremacy and the curiously co-related rise of Jewish racism; Wagner's use of incest as a symbolic expression of the synthesis of complementary principles necessary for the world's survival; his exploration of what Jean Paul called "that inner Africa," the unconscious. Dr. Rather makes confident and competent use of Sophocles, Feuerbach, Kant, Heine, Schopenhauer, Hegel, Marx, and—muddy Wagnerian waters indeed!—Gobineau and Chamberlain. Though the author may sound, from this description, like a wide-eyed Stanley in search of a hyped-up Livingstone, what he says is in fact carefully researched and soberly argued. He also provides a startlingly unorthodox bibliography.

Shaw, George Bernard, *The Perfect Wagnerite: A Commentary on the Niblung's* [sic] *Ring* (New York: Dover Publications, 1967, originally published in 1898). An early, seriously witty attempt to find political and economic dimensions in the *Ring*. Donington rightly remarks that Shaw "mingles great sense and great silliness in about equal proportions," but of course the opinionated Shaw knew when he was being silly and when sensible, and expected us to know the difference.

Spencer, Stewart, and Millington, Barry, trans. and eds., *Selected Letters of Richard Wagner* (New York: W. W. Norton, 1987). New, eminently readable translations of five hundred of Wagner's twelve thousand letters, including those to August Röckel and Franz Liszt that are indispensable for an understanding of the *Ring*. A volume we have needed for a long time, superbly edited.

Recordings

VIDEO

Bayreuth Festival production, <u>1979–80</u>. Conducted by Pierre Boulez. Staged by Patrice Chéreau. Eleven laser discs (Philips 070–501/4–1). With Donald MacIntyre (Wotan), Gwyneth Jones (Brünnhilde), Manfred Jung (Siegfried), Jeannine Altmeyer and Peter Hofmann (Sieglinde and Siegmund), Hermann Becht (Alberich).

First staged for the Bayreuth centenary in <u>1976</u>. Hailed and hated then, and thought to be innovative and iconoclastic, it seems on film and disc to do little more by way of novelty than to put <u>Shaw</u>'s eighty-year-old interpretation (the <u>Ring</u> as metaphor for the Industrial Revolution) on the Bayreuth stage. Musically it is, on the whole, badly sung and feebly played. Boulez consistently sacrifices Wagner's musical intent to underline Chéreau's Shavian scenics. Joseph Kerman rightly called the whole a "programmatically controversial and basically foolish production."

On the other hand there is no denying that Chéreau is phenomenally successful in coaxing good, not to say great, acting performances from singers. In previous decades at Bayreuth, under Wieland Wagner, acting was stylized, as characters were ranged across a raked stage in pools of light and darkness, and the spatial relationships between them defined their psychological states. In time, this remarkable style was too widely imitated across Europe, and "neo-Bayreuth" became a cliché in productions even of Shakespeare and Schiller. Chéreau changed all that to introduce realistic, passionate, utterly convincing acting. In 1976 most people had never seen such forceful drama on an operatic—perhaps on any—stage. It was a triumphant vindication of Wagner's genius. Much of the effect of this— a stunned Wotan looking into his dying son's eyes and acknowledging him for the first time, a grieving Brünnhilde caught like some flailing, helpless white bird between a Siegfried she no longer knows and a Gunther she cannot understand—is captured on video in expressive close-ups and medium shots that shut out the intrusive silliness of the Shavian sets and partly compensate for the limpness of the musical performance.

NOTE: The Metropolitan Opera will telecast the cycle complete in June of 1990, in the production by Otto Schenk and Günther Schneider-Siemssen, with James Levine conducting and with James Morris, Hildegard Behrens, Siegfried Jerusalem, Jessye Norman, and Gary Lakes in leading roles. In the theater, this was an often overwhelming experience. Levine had the Metropolitan Opera orchestra playing like one of the world's greatest, and drew some stunning vocal performances from his singers. Naturalistic settings close to Wagner's original intentions allowed viewers to feel their way into the cycle's myriad meanings without being confronted and affronted by the spurious superimpositions found in most contemporary inscenations. Surely Wagner's scenic expectations for the final moments of Götterdämmerung have never been so completely realized on any other stage. How much of this will be captured on video and laser disc remains, at this writing, to be seen.

AUDIO

As most of the following have made their way onto CD, I shall list them without their various LP and 78 serial numbers.

Sir Georg Solti, conductor. *London/Decca*. Fifteen CDs (London 414 100-2 LM-15), now digitally remastered. With George London/Hans Hotter (W), Birgit Nilsson (B), Wolfgang Windgassen (S), Régine Crespin and James King (S and S), Gustav Neidlinger (A). The Vienna Philharmonic Orchestra.

First issued on LP in 1958–66. Studio-produced by the far-sighted John Culshaw, this first *Ring* for the phonograph remains a milestone in recording history. As a performance it is often very exciting and, considering the long time span required for its realization, of a remarkably even consistency, with strong vocal contributions. Solti's conducting is manic and grandiloquent. Some listeners find it short on poetry, which only proves that there is more than one approach to Wagner's *magnum opus*. For poetry see the next entry.

Herbert von Karajan, conductor. *Deutsche Grammophon*. Fifteen CDs (DG 415141, 415145, 415150, 415155), now digitally remastered. With Dietrich Fischer-Dieskau/ Thomas Stewart (W), Régine Crespin/Helga Dernesch (B), Jess Thomas/Helge Brilioth (S), Gundula Janowitz and Jon Vickers (S and S), Zoltán Kélemen (A). The Berlin Philharmonic Orchestra.

First issued on LP in 1966–70. Karajan achieves more elegance of line and more beautifully textured studio sound than did his predecessor Solti, and with his obedient and less high-powered singers, well into their roles after a series of live performances at Salzburg, he almost turns the *Ring* into a quietly introspective drama interrupted only occasionally by climactic moments.

Karl Böhm, conductor. *Philips.* Fourteen CDs (Philips 412475, 412478, 412483, 412488), now digitally remastered. With Theo Adam (W), Birgit Nilsson (B), Wolfgang Windgassen (S), Leonie Rysanek and James King (S and S), Gustav Neidlinger (A). The Bayreuth Festival Orchestra.

First issued on LP in 1966–67. A fast-paced, sometimes reckless live performance (the Wieland Wagner production of the mid-sixties) in which many of the singers Solti used are driven by Böhm to new heights of dramatic intensity. The Bayreuth acoustic creates on disc a sound quite different from that of the two previous issues, an ambience in which singers and orchestra blend without studioesque enhancement.

Marek Janowski, conductor. *Eurodisc.* Eighteen CDs (6100–5823, 6423, 7023, 8123). With Theo Adam (W), Jeannine Altmeyer (B), René Kollo (S), Jessye Norman and Siegfried Jerusalem (S and S), Siegmund Nimsgern (A). The Dresden State Orchestra.

First issued on LP/CD in 1980–83 (the first digitally recorded studio *Ring* and also the first to appear on CD), this attractive performance is a cut below the others, though Janowski conducts with uncommon attention to detail and gets the singers to sound much surer than they do in the same roles in the theater.

NOTE: Both EMI and Deutsche Grammophon are currently in the process of recording the cycle complete, the former with the Bavarian Radio Orchestra under Bernard Haitink, the latter with Metropolitan Opera forces under James Levine. Both feature James Morris as Wotan amid spectacular state-of-the-art sound.

A SELECTIVE LIST OF OLDER RECORDINGS

Hans Knappertsbusch, conductor. *Music and Arts.* Fifteen CDs (CD–253–256). With Hans Hotter (W), Astrid Varnay (B), Bernd Aldenhoff/Wolfgang Windgassen (S), Birgit Nilsson and Ramón Vinay (S and S), Gustav Neidlinger (A).

First issued on LP in 1978. Recorded live at Bayreuth in 1957, this monophonic performance is important mainly to the collector. Tempi are monumental, often sluggishly so, and the singers are heard to better advantage on other recordings. See the next entry.

Clemens Krauss, conductor. *Harmonia Mundi (Rodolphe Productions).* Seven CDs (RPC 32503–9). Also available, with digital remastering, on *Foyer/Laudis,* fifteen CDs (15–CF–2011). With Hans Hotter (W), Astrid Varnay (B), Wolfgang Windgassen (S), Regina Resnik and Ramón Vinay (S and S), Gustav Neidlinger (A).

First issued on CD in 1988. Recorded live at Bayreuth in 1953, this monophonic performance has been channeled by Rodolphe onto left and right tracks separately and thus occupies less than half the CD space required by other complete recordings. (The company supplies an adapter for buyers with less than sophisticated equipment.) The sound on the Foyer/Laudis is, however, preferable, and at mid-price its fifteen discs are a good investment, as an increasing number of Wagnerians are coming to regard this as the greatest *Ring* on records, with a conductor in the grand tradition and a cast of singers actually surpassing the fine performances they give on other recordings.

Wilhelm Furtwängler, conductor. *Fonit Cetra.* Fourteen CDs (CDC 26, 15, 27, 28). With Ferdinand Frantz/Josef Herrmann (W), Kirsten Flagstad (B), Set Svanholm/Max Lorenz (S), Hilde Konetzni and Günther Treptow (S and S), Alois Pernerstorfer (A).

There have been two *Ring* cycles on disc conducted by Wilhelm Furtwängler. One, which has not yet appeared on CD, stems from live broadcasts from Rome's RAI studio, with a less than first-rate orchestra, in 1953. The other, cited here, is taken from stage performances at La Scala in 1950. Even with two fairly lengthy cuts, variable sound, a good deal of audience noise, and an opera house orchestra not fully into the Wagner tradition, this will be for many the first choice among *Ring* recordings—especially for Kirsten Flagstad's superb Brünnhilde and for conducting that continues the great central European tradition extending back through Mahler and Nikisch to Seidl and Richter. Furtwängler builds steadily in great arcs of sound, with pacing that seems infallibly right.

EXCERPTS

Act I of *Die Walküre* received its finest realization on disc in 1935 when Bruno Walter conducted it with the Vienna Philharmonic and Lotte Lehmann, Lauritz Melchior, and Emanuel List. Has any other Sieglinde's voice ever brimmed so with rapture, joy, and pride in her Siegmund? This is the stuff dreams are made of. Now available on a single digitally remastered CD from EMI: CDH 7 61020 2, in the series appropriately titled Great Recordings of the Century.

From 1927 to 1932 Lauritz Melchior recorded an extensive series of excerpts from *Siegfried* under several conductors and with such fine colleagues as Florence Easton, Friedrich Schorr, and Rudolf Bockelmann. The listener soon feels that, over a century, only Melchior has sung the young hero's demanding music with the requisite musicianship, vividness of characterization, and stamina. Now available on three CDs from Danacord: DACOCD 319–321.

Arturo Toscanini, in a series of broadcasts and studio recordings made over several years, conducted orchestral and vocal excerpts from the *Ring* with the New York Philharmonic, the NBC Symphony, Lauritz Melchior, and Helen Traubel. His incandescent, uniquely songlike conducting is at variance with the Germanic tradition Furtwängler was continuing so eloquently at much the same time, and the relative merits of the two great conductors are still argued *ad infinitum* by Wagnerians. In recent years the scales have dipped decidedly in favor of Furtwängler, but Wagnerians of Ernest Newman's day almost consistently said that the greatest Wagner performances they ever heard were those under Toscanini at Bayreuth. The excerpts have had a long life on 78 and LP, and will almost surely appear soon on CD. But the perennial argument between partisans of the two conductors could only be settled if a complete Toscanini *Ring* were to turn up on disc. Unfortunately that bit of history was never made.

Index of Musical Themes

Though I have presumed to give names to the following examples, it must be stressed that Wagner himself thought of the two hundred or so musical themes in the Ring not as tags identifying personages, objects, and ideas so much as "motifs of memory." Themes that in Das Rheingold carry simple associations are by the end of the cycle charged with additional meaning from their recurrent interaction with one another and with the text and staging.

EXAMPLE 1: The primal element

EXAMPLE 2: Water (from the primal element)

EXAMPLE 3: Earth (from the primal element)

EXAMPLE 4: Reversion to the primal element

EXAMPLE 5: Water murmurs

EXAMPLE 6: Forest murmurs

EXAMPLE 7: Water cries

EXAMPLE 8: Forest cries

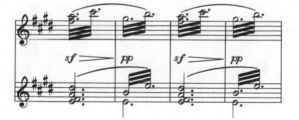

EXAMPLE 9: Song of the water maidens

EXAMPLE 10: Song of the forest bird

EXAMPLE 11: The Rhine gold

EXAMPLE 12: The sword

EXAMPLE 13: World enslavement

EXAMPLE 14: World enslavement (developed)

EXAMPLE 15: World release

EXAMPLE 16: The moment of choice

EXAMPLE 17: The spear

EXAMPLE 18: Valhalla

EXAMPLE 19: The Ring

EXAMPLE 20: Brünnhilde's plea (the spear)

EXAMPLE 21: Wotan's response (the spear)

EXAMPLE 22: Brünnhilde

EXAMPLE 23: Siegfried

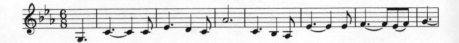

EXAMPLE 24: Slumber

About the Author

FATHER OWEN LEE is a professor of Classics at St. Michael's College at the University of Toronto. The author of books on Horace and Virgil as well as more than a hundred articles on both classical and musical subjects, he teaches not only Greek and Latin poetry but courses on comparative literature, art, music, and film. He is a frequent guest on the intermission features of the Met/Texaco radio broadcasts.